Bold
is beautiful

KINDNESS, BEAUTY AND STRENGTH

COMPILED BY

KIM BOUDREAU SMITH

Bold is Beautiful

Coaching and Success
c/o Marketing for Coach, Ltd
Second Floor
6th London Street
W2 1HR London (UK)

www.coachingandsuccess.com
info@coachingandsuccess.com

ISBN: 978-0-9575561-5-7

Published in UK, Europe, US and Canada

Book Cover: Alvaro Beleza

Inside Layout: Alvaro Beleza

TABLE OF CONTENTS

OREWORD
by Christine Marmoy

Being "bold" actually means so much more than we tend to use the term for! Even though we are rapidly approaching the year 2014, women across the globe still face many difficulties today when it comes to being on the outside who they truly are on the inside.

This hindrance interferes with all aspects of their lives. Sometimes it creates confusion and doubt in their relationships, their channels of communication get broken, their dreams are left shattered and achieving self-love and self-esteem is almost impossible.

When Kim first showed me the photo she wanted to use for her cover, I just fell in love with it at first sight because to me it embodied Kim's vision exactly. Every woman is golden, every woman is bold inside – whether or not she lets that golden glow shine through. And that is Kim's mission. She has the talent to see beyond the masks you wear; she can very easily tap into your essence even if you have kept it buried for years. Kim's vision with this book was to present at least a chosen few with the opportunity to shine a ray of golden light onto our world, to break free from the self-imposed greyness in which so many of them were imprisoned.

And I'm delighted to say that she succeeded brilliantly in her quest. This book is the proof that all of you are golden, that all of you have a message to share. Throughout the creation of this project, Kim and I were bowled over by the transformation some of these co-authors went through. It was a real journey and one that will have permanent effects.

This book is a direct reflection of what Kim is all about. It's fresh, punchy, smart, heart-centered while being very true and honest. Kim deeply cares! She cares about all the women out there hiding behind the false belief that they aren't good enough or special enough to be who they really are. Kim has the ability to make them stand up to that and face it head-on in a strong and bold way. She is the sounding board so many of you have been looking for.

She is also a fervent believer and advocate of clear and strong actions; this is how she handles her business and her life. This is also the reason why she is so successful. This project was one of her strong actions; she decided upon it, she set it in motion, now it is published.

Strong actions, yes – bold actions, absolutely, but that's not just it… everything Kim puts forward is filled with love, passion, care and a deep sense of responsibility.

Many women in business are failing miserably because they do not believe in themselves enough to put themselves out there, to market their business, to share their message in a more impactful manner. If that is you, I'm so glad you picked up this book because you are in for a real treat. You are all beautiful Souls in your own right; this is what Kim wants to share with you through her book. It's your birthright; nobody can take that away from you.

Reclaim your authenticity, decide today that you are deserving of and worthy of shining your light so you can make a real difference in your business as much as in your life.

Reading through the following pages, you'll recognize yourself in each of these women's stories. Each one of them could be your own story.

APPRECIATION AND GRATITUDE

First of all I would like to begin by saying that the words "thank you" feel so shallow, light and not deep enough to what I really feel. I stand in such gratitude for *Bold is Beautiful* coming to fruition! One year ago, I would never have said I wanted to compile a book, but my experience becoming an international best-selling author in April 2013 was an elating and exuberant experience, so I decided to share this feeling and opportunity with 29 other women. (And, of course, not to mention sharing with the world!)

So I begin with gratitude and the most heartfelt thank you to the 29 amazing women, the co-authors of *Bold is Beautiful*, that you will soon meet as you turn these pages; these women are bold and so beautiful! My dream of *Bold is Beautiful* could not have become a reality without these women. I am in such gratitude to each and every one of you. Your boldness is so beautiful, inside and out. A few of you are great personal friends that I have met through different venues, and for some of you, our meeting in person still awaits us; however, the connection we all have grown is priceless, and it has only just begun.

To my circle sisters in my life: I am so deeply appreciative to all of you beautiful women. The gift that is given by each and every one of you is beyond any words imaginable that I can express. Ellen, a large part of me is here today because of your love, growth, passion and huge vision! I love you all.

To my many mentors in my life from teachers to coaches and great friends, I am in gratitude for your leadership, insights, support and listening ears. You know who you are. Gratitude goes to my colleagues,

11

past clients and current clients and Facebook contacts that have supported me, "liked" my posts and shown their amazing light. You all are wonderful!

A special appreciation for Christine Marmoy and her support, understanding and being a kick-ass friend who pushes me to unlimited heights as I grow and continue to be Bold! Also, for your gift of kind and bold words for the foreword of this book, thank you. You see such greatness in me.

In gratitude for my parents, they showed me that playing small is not an option.

Last, but not of course least, my husband Steve. You are the most supportive man I know. You are so instrumental for where I am today. I know that I am not the easiest person to live with, but we do have fun, and yes you can drive me crazy, too. I love you! I love your excitement with my accomplishments and your excitement for the co-authors as well. You are so kind, considerate and you really "get all of this." I remember coming to you about the book and your response was "why wouldn't you?" and "of course you are going to do this!" Steve, I appreciate and I am grateful for you.

To my four-legged office assistants, Koda and Grace, they are the bosses of my office. Koda, who continually sleeps on the job and Grace who reminds me it's time to take a break. I love you both, my girls!

Now let's get to the book and meet those beautiful and bold co-authors! Enjoy.

$\mathcal{I}$NTRODUCTION

I remember the day when Christine Marmoy lightly said, "Kim you should compile a book." Well I laughed and said, "I am not a writer, I am a talker!" This was shortly after I became an international best-selling author with *Success in High Heels*. Well, I had no idea how my life would change in such a short amount of time. Of course I laughed at her. Well, one morning I woke up and the words "Bold is Beautiful" came to me. I just carried them with me for a while. Then Christine spoke again more seriously about a book, visibility, and creating opportunity for 29 other women, and I knew right then and there that "Bold is Beautiful" needed to be a book.

My vision was to bring together a community of women from around the world to connect, share, grow and form a bond of sisterhood. These women have different walks of life, careers, spirituality, so you the reader can relate in many different ways.

This was a bold step for me, but I knew from the support of Christine and my husband, I had to do this. It is about paying forward the same opportunity that Christine provided for me; I really wanted the same for 29 other women from around the world! A complete no-brainer for me. I love creating opportunity for other women.

One by one these women showed up – on Facebook, in my community, and referrals from other women.

Each co-author has opened their hearts to you, to share what it is like to BE – to truly discover one's self and fall in love with one's self going deeper and really making changes in their lives. The tears, the loss, the un-knowing, but the inner guidance to keep moving forward;

to become more confident, stronger for themselves as well as their families and other women around the world!

Bold is Beautiful and yes, this is every woman from the inside out, bold and gold. I so admire the strengths of these women; they share what it has taken to arrive to who their "being" is today. I was left speechless with the stories. I laughed, I cried and I took deep breaths, as I read each and every story.

This book is birthed from our hearts, and it is a way to provide hope to all of you reading this book. I believe every woman should never give up hope on anything. Gather your village of support, like these women did.

The world as known today is about women stepping up into their dreams and changing the mindset, habits, behaviors and patterns to become your bold self! It is time for women to lead alongside other women and men as well. Enough of playing small. Go for it, the world is yours!

This project began with the sentiment that I do not want any women or men to ever feel alone again. I come from a background with a lack of self-worth and living lies to be accepted. No More! I hope you can take away a golden nugget or many golden nuggets for YOU! Ladies, no more losing hope, no more quitting, or giving up, never again! These ladies didn't give up. They kept moving forward to pay it forward for others. This is where the "I cant's" end and change to the "I can!" Get rid of the "it's too late." No, it is not. If you are still alive it is never too late to start or to change.

Despite my fears and stepping out of a comfort zone, you now have this book in your hands. You see being Bold is so Beautiful! Please use this book to move you forward, provide hope and feel like a part of community. We all want to hear of your Bold Successes.

– *Kim Boudreau Smith*

Business consultant & strategist, speaker,
international best-selling author and
proprietor of Bold Radio Station

KIM BOUDREAU SMITH

Kim is an international business consultant & strategist, speaker and international best-selling author.

Kim's company, Kim Boudreau Smith, Inc., is dedicated to supporting women entrepreneurs to step into living their dream lives! To step stronger into their Bold selves, become top producers in their life and achieve the wanted results – success! Kim teaches women how to sell like a woman, with love and integrity!

Helping over 1,000 people successfully achieve healthier lifestyles with her first business, she is taking this extensive business knowledge and paying it forward – helping women entrepreneurs defy obstacles, stop settling for less, step into their boldness and enjoy success.

Kim is a passionate believer in collaboration, providing opportunities for other women and has a desire to motivate and support others to achieve their best through taking a call to action and achieving extraordinary results.

✉ kim@kimboudreausmith.com

⌂ www.kimbsmith.com

⌂ www.boldradiostation.com

🎙 www.blogtalkradio.com/leadherupisin

f www.facebook.com/kboudreausmith

BOLD IS BEAUTIFUL

- **www.facebook.com/KimBoudreauSmith**
- **www.linkedin.com/in/kimboudreausmith**
- **twitter.com/KimBSmithInc**

CHAPTER I

YOU ARE TO BE SEEN AND NOT HEARD!

By Kim Boudreau Smith

As a child our worlds are created and molded by our parents, and then when we grow older and go to school, teachers start defining us as well. As we grow further into adulthood, we start defining ourselves, molding ourselves into what society thinks we should be, then we gather up limiting beliefs from others in our careers, friends, and the environment. We make up stories and buy into the stories, failures and scarcity and then we live lives of unhappiness that lack authenticity!

When I was young I was a very shy child (if you know me you are either laughing and saying, "yea, right,"). I was quiet and didn't dare talk "out of turn." My mother raised me to be respectful, so I was to be seen and not heard. When it was time to go to school, I was petrified to speak. This became a problem and concern for my mom (Yes, the one who told me to been seen and not heard then became concerned about my "shyness"). I realized very early in life that if I spoke up, I was bossy, I had a big mouth or I was disrespectful. Talk about limiting beliefs, wow!

At the age of 7, my parents enrolled me in dance lessons to bring me out of my shell and to build confidence. The once a week dance lessons turned into twice a week, performing on many stages with a lot of costume changes and also competing for state titles. I tried out for the Dance Club in high school (against my better judgment, I did this for my friends, which is another story), and the teacher told me that I was terrible and would never make it as a dancer. Ha! I had been dancing for 9 years at this point. You see, what is told to us at any point in our lives is not true. We are the creators of our own stories – our lives; it is what we choose to filter into our thoughts, which become our habits, and, in turn, to our behaviors.

Do you hold on to limiting beliefs from your childhood? I know I did for quite some time. Actually, I held on so tight that I talked myself asleep at a major intersection! It wasn't just my actual voice, it was the voice inside my head that I let rule me. I silenced my actual voice by saying things I thought others wanted to hear for acceptance. I silenced my voice in my heart and my intuitive voice as well – the real me, my true voice. This led me down a path of great corporate success (so I thought) and a failed first marriage. I got married because of the societal voice telling me I should be married! However, I wasn't happy, but I thought I was successful. And when the corporate thing fell apart, I discovered what a downward spiral I was on; however, this didn't stop me from proving people wrong about me!

I grew up in a normal middle class family with fears and many restrictions, so when I left corporate America and took a leap to start my first business, I was going against the norm. Who was going to pay for my health insurance, where was the paycheck going to come from? Money doesn't grow on trees! What about retirement? I always felt so restricted, so I had to prove to my parents that I could be successful in corporate with a title and money, and also prove them wrong that being self-employed / owning a business can be profitable and I could make money.

Well, I will tell you that I created great momentum at first, then things would slow down, but being the go-getter than I am, I would create programs and they would sell out, then things would get slow again. On again, off again – very overwhelming and frustrating. I thought I would lose my mind. It felt like I was always looking for clients and consistency. I was holding on to so many beliefs. This became an ongoing pattern in my life even with my health. I was losing sleep, stressed out and continuously worried about money. My thoughts consumed me, and I was receiving exactly what I focused on.

Now, don't get me wrong, I had a very successful business, but something was always lacking. I had no idea this was the best thing

I could have done for myself and what success was ahead of me. Several years later I fell asleep at a major intersection during the day. No one was hurt, but I knew that my thoughts had to change. I spoke myself into a slumber. I had not even begun to reach my full success in life. At this point, I had 48 years of brainwashing to undo and an endless amount of limiting beliefs to attend to. I was ready to push up my sleeves and get down to business – the business of ME! This was going to be like having open-heart surgery, changing my thoughts and so much more.

Being bold is about making a decision and moving forward on it. It's about recognizing the bitch in the attic (our inner self critic/ego) IS NOT our true selves. Changing those thoughts that have limited us for years and held us back from our inner dreams and beauty has to happen. When you can admit and become aware that your patterns and habits are not working for you, then they must be changed. It's giving something up. For me, it was giving up the fake me. Boy, she was a tough one to overcome, believe me. I was willing to give this all up to feel my joy, success, and serenity. I was an anxious mess. My business was failing. I didn't even have a desire or passion to get up out of bed, let alone get through the day.

So off I went on my transformation journey, which included my business. I became a certified life coach, created The I-Academy, teen empowerment programs, Business Consulting for Women Entrepreneurs, started speaking, became an international best-selling author (multiple times), and I own an Internet radio Station, Bold Radio. Oh, by the way, my first business is a fitness business that is still alive and running (no pun intended!).

My reason for these 3 businesses is:

1. So women don't have to take as long to create a profitable business,

2. To support others in managing the mindset to be their bold and successful selves, and

3. To be able to travel internationally through speaking engagements and workshops.

This was no easy journey. I had a lot to let go of and change 48 years worth of stories and limiting beliefs that kept me small. I had to speak my true voice.

Being bold is getting comfortable with being uncomfortable, taking risks and a few slaps on the face (yes, those still sting and hurt) along the way, as well as falling down. I see the golden boldness in every woman weather she sees this in herself or not. It takes work changing those beliefs, but it is so much more freeing and empowering. I could not see all of this, especially in others, if I had not changed up my thoughts and my own beliefs.

By the way, I am not done. This is work in progress; it is a marathon, not "hurry and let's get to the finish line." This takes time, and the first step is to acknowledge and become aware of where you are in this very moment. This is the very beginning of any process – becoming aware and then having the desire to change. Remember, there will always be obstacles, some in your mind and some as a part of your environment. Again, the first step is acknowledging this, and then getting real serious about solving or changing the belief, then getting past the setbacks. Your inner voice will get louder before becoming quieter; it's part of the process. Seems easy, right? Remember you are unwinding several years here, so get yourself some support!

My reason to take on an Internet radio station is for other women to be heard through their voices, without limiting beliefs, to speak internationally and make a difference around the world, through their amazing voices.

Places to begin changing your thoughts:

- Meditation – begin small, 10 minutes a day

- Workout – take a walk outside, which is a great way to clear the cobwebs from the brain

- "I am" positive affirmation statements

- Surround yourself with like-minded individuals

You have taken your first step by holding and reading this book. Now don't stop, do not turn back, and keep moving forward.

Make sure you are giving this "your all." I tell my clients a minimum of ninety days is needed for a habit to change.

Now, I want to hear from you. Email me to share your Bold yet Beautiful self. The world is waiting, don't waste another second!

BOLD IS BEAUTIFUL

NICOLE EASTMAN, D.O.

Dr. Nicole M. Eastman turned to therapeutic writing and ministry through her website, www.drnicolemeastman.com, following a near-fatal car accident in December 2010. Prior to her accident, she earned her degree in medicine from Michigan State University College of Osteopathic Medicine, East Lansing, Michigan. Prior to medicine, she earned her Bachelor of Science in Psychology from Wayne State University, Detroit, Michigan. Throughout her undergraduate studies she worked many jobs, including employment as a NASM and ACE certified personal trainer and AFAA certified group fitness instructor. Currently, Dr. Eastman resides in Grand Cayman with her husband, Tim, and their beautiful son, Jack.

🏠 www.drnicolemeastman.com

f Facebook Pages: Dr. Nicole M. Eastman (Writer):
www.facebook.com/pages/Dr-Nicole-M-Eastman-DO/226755637390614

f Motor Vehicle Accident Survivors Facebook Page:
www.facebook.com/pages/Motor-Vehicle-Accident-Survivors/289911374379121

f Brain Injury Awareness Month Facebook Page:
www.facebook.com/BrainInjuryAwarenessMonth

f www.twitter.com/DrNicoleEastman

in www.linkedin.com/pub/dr-nicole-eastman-d-o/36/b5/a8a/

23

✉ nicolemeastman1@gmail.com

Ⓢ Skype: Nicole Eastman (timnicoleeastman)

Current Residence:
Grand Cayman, Cayman Islands
Cayman Phone Number: 1-345-928-0897

CHAPTER 2

$\mathscr{C}$OURAGE TO MOVE

By Nicole Eastman, D.O.

Move forward, that is – the courage to move forward. Those words sure are easier to say now that I am entering a new season in life. You see, for the past several years, my life has been filled with a great amount of physical and psychological pain, overwhelming loss, and undesirable feelings of hopelessness and despair. "It would have been easier to die than to survive and go through what I am going through every day" are words that were felt and expressed during some of my darkest moments. Those moments were surrounded by uncontrollable events that led to the loss of everything that I had worked so hard to achieve.

So, what brought about this season of pain and suffering? Let me take you back in time with me to the year 2010. I was at the start of my career as an osteopathic doctor. I had just graduated from Michigan State University College of Osteopathic Medicine, and I was expecting to complete a residency in rehabilitation medicine. On November 26, 2010, I married my husband in beautiful Grand Cayman, which is the largest of three islands located in the Cayman Islands. Although my father had passed away in 2008, his spiritual presence was with me; and, his presence was honored with a bouquet of beautiful orchids that sat on the chair next to my mother during our ceremony. My two brothers walked me down the aisle to Pachelbel in D and then, they both gave their approval to the man who was about to become my husband. Following our wedding vows, we moved on to enjoy our reception at Grand Old House, which had been completely transformed into a scene of tropical elegance. There was so much to celebrate in life! I was 29 years old, I had already achieved so much, and it felt like life was just beginning.

We returned back to Michigan and only two weeks later, let me repeat that, only two weeks following our "for better for worse" and our "in sickness and in health" vows. Then, our marriage was tested and it was tested big time. On December 15, 2010, I was driving to work when my life almost came to an abrupt end. All it took was an extreme force from behind to send my car, a 2004 Chrysler Sebring Sedan, and my life spinning. My car was rear-ended by a semi-truck, not once, not twice, but what appears from photos to have been four times at nearly 65 mile per hour. I recall being hit from behind, my car spinning counterclockwise, seeing the large red semi-truck coming towards my driver's side door, being hit the second time near my car's gas tank, and then, I remember facing oncoming traffic - with my teeth clenched and my thoughts turned to God, my deceased father, and the patients who I had come into contact with who had been affected by brain and spine injuries. I didn't want to endure what those people had experienced. I expected that I was going to die; and, I wondered what death was going to be like. I didn't know what to expect, but I did not expect to live. However, by the grace of God, I survived.

I survived, but the person who I once was, definitely died. Following my accident, I went through denial and then, depression as realizations became more apparent and I continued to experience loss. I experienced the effects of a concussion, spinal damage, spinal surgery, post-traumatic stress, and pain, which still to this day, is present on a daily basis. I experienced feeling all alone, great marital strife, and an outer appearance that was and still is, quite deceiving. I experienced grief, frustration, and anger; and with time and faith, I then, came to experience acceptance and healing. As I look back, I realize that none of this healing would have been possible without courage.

For me, courage came in many forms. It is my hope that through sharing these, that you too can define areas in your own life that will allow you further growth.

- **Courage to Accept Defeat**. Following my accident I broke down to the lowest point of my entire life, and I felt completely defeated. Depression consumed me as each of my previously constructed walls, which served as protection from any possible form of hurt, were demolished. How terrifying that was; because, once those walls were removed, I could see my weaknesses, I could feel my emotions, and I could realize my vulnerability.

- **Courage to Accept Faith.** I was raised Catholic and throughout my life, I believed in God; however, I never had a deep relationship within my faith. It wasn't until I felt completely alone, was lying in bed overwhelmed with pain, and filled with feelings of hopelessness, that I realized that I was not alone. I had God. From that moment forward, my relationship in Christ began to grow. My husband and I started attending Macomb Christian Church in Shelby Township, Michigan, where we both accepted and received forgiveness through baptism; and, as my marriage was tested over and over again, it was my love for God, which kept me united to my husband. Through prayer, meditation, and counsel from trusted ministers, I came to the understanding that God was now using me as His vessel to reach others who desperately needed to feel His love.

- **Courage to Receive.** Prior to my accident, I took pride in self-sufficiency. I was great at giving, but receiving, that was a different story. Due to the accident, however, I had to learn to accept help and to receive. This was tortuous at times; and, it was a source of more marital distress. No husband expects to become a caretaker to his physically active, overachieving, hyper-independent, and professionally successful wife; and no woman of this type desires to be taken care of. This, however, was exactly what we were facing. My husband's new responsibilities included household chores and physically assisting me following my spine surgery. For weeks he had to administer my medicine, he pretty much carried me in and out of bed to use the restroom, he held me up so I could shower, and he stayed by my side despite the efforts of others to get him to leave. For my husband, he received the gift of being able to give. The gift that I received was the ability to accept love.

- **Courage to Find Myself.** Following a period of denial and depression, I became increasingly aware of the fact that I no longer knew who "I" was. So much of our identity seems to be rooted in our achievements and with the great loss I suffered, I lost my sense of self. This too caused considerable pain, and this pain was a catalyst to a new journey of self-exploration and self-discovery.

- **Courage to Grieve.** Although my father passed away in 2008, it took me 3 years to appropriately grieve his loss. It wasn't until my life was forced to slow down that I was able to come to terms with my feelings. In addition to grieving his death, I grieved the death of the person that I was prior to my accident. No longer could I relate to who I once was, because every single aspect of my life had been altered in a matter of seconds beyond my control.

- **Courage to Be Vulnerable.** Writing became part of my therapy. The pain that I had experienced turned into a passion for helping others; helping those who feel like I once did – all alone. My mission to spread God's love has allowed me the strength to share my testimony. Although this has left me vulnerable, it has also allowed me healing; and, as I have healed, others have too.

- **Courage to Let Go.** This included letting go of unhealthy habits and unhealthy relationships. Letting go of the negativity was critical to self-preservation. In order to manage my pain, it became absolutely a must to maintain a positive environment. This initially caused more distress, however, I am grateful that I survived the initial backlash and have been able to maintain these positive changes.

- **Courage to Embrace Uncertainty.** I once perceived uncertainty as terrifying; however, I now see it as an opportunity. I used to feel like I was in control of my life, but I have come to learn that we have a very false perception of control. There is a plan much greater than our own, so when my husband and I felt led to make a move, we did. Nearing my third trimester of pregnancy, my husband and I sold most of our material belongings and we moved to Grand Cayman. I never imagined that I could move out of Michigan, let alone out of the country, but that is exactly what we did. Despite our own fear and the fear expressed by others, we took a huge leap of faith and began a new chapter of life together – one with more challenges and hardships, but more so, one with amazing growth.

- **Courage to Trust**. By this, I mean trusting in God and His plan. It means praising Him in the good times and in times of trial. There is great power in prayer.

- **Courage to Heal**. Part of the journey to healing has to do with personal choice and attitude. I recently read a quote from Joyce Meyer Ministries that said, "God helps those who help themselves." This I find to be true. You have a choice to move forward or to stay stuck in the past, to allow yourself peace and positivity or to become entangled in negativity, to grow or remain defeated, and to trust in God and receive His great power of healing or to continue to think you can do it all on your own.

I declare that this season of pain and suffering is ending and that I am entering a new season – a season of joy. Although this last season of life leaves me with many hidden realities, I have learned what it means to rejoice in my suffering. I am who I have become, because of my experiences; and, I am grateful for the lessons learned and the growth received through my times of trial.

BOLD IS BEAUTIFUL

CELIA SETZER

Celia Setzer is 57 years old. She has dedicated her life to God and her family. Writing has always been a great passion for Celia. She has spent her life raising her children and enriching her marriage of 27 years. Now that her children are grown, she is able to spend more time writing. Her story is about a mother's love and the battle she fought to keep her son. In writing this chapter, Celia hopes to encourage mothers to fight for what's right. It doesn't take a lot of money, just a strong love for your children.

 setzercelia@gmail.com

CHAPTER 3

THE HEART'S REASON

By Celia Setzer

In 1977 I was married, I had a four-year-old daughter and I was nine months pregnant. My husband was killed in a terrible car wreck. My mind totally went into a state of shock. The day of my husband's funeral I went into labor. I was in full force labor. My parents drove me to the hospital when my pains were five minutes apart. At the hospital, the pains started to come closer and closer. Around midnight or so, my labor stopped. The doctor kept me overnight and gave me a shot of something to make me rest and to make sure my baby was ok.

Two days later I went into labor for real this time, and I had my son. He was healthy and weighed 8 pounds and 6 ounces. I had no feelings whatsoever. After I left the hospital I stayed with my parents for a few days. Then I moved in with my deceased husband's parents for a couple months. During this time, my mother-in law would come in my room early in the morning and take my son to her room where they would play with him, and because of my state of mind my son bonded with her. I just thought I was helping them with their grief of losing their son.

After a few weeks I moved into a small furnished apartment with just our clothes and a baby bed. I had gone back to work and my kids went to their grandma's while I was at work. Still not allowing myself to feel the pain, I would work to keep my mind busy. I started going to the bars, and would leave the kids at their Grandma's. I was unfit to have my kids with me. I stayed drunk all the time so I didn't have to deal with losing my husband. His parents wanted my son, but there never was anything mentioned about my daughter when it came to who was to have custody of her. All they wanted was my son.

When my son was about six months old I had moved his bed around and when doing this, one of the corners a came apart. He rolled down into the gap and was stuck. When I was getting him out, his leg got caught and it broke. I didn't know. I thought he was crying because he was scared. I thought he had picked up on me being scared.

When he was almost a year old I had met a man that was crazy over my kids. After going to bed I woke up to my son crying. I went to check on him and my boyfriend said he was ok and for me to go back to bed. A few days later my son started running a fever. I thought he was just cutting teeth. His fever got higher and I made him a doctor's appointment. My mother-in-law met us there. We sat and waited a long time, and I had to go to work so my mother-in-law said she would let me know what was going on. I waited for a while and didn't hear anything, so I called the doctor's office, and the lady told me the police had been called along with the welfare people. My son's leg was swollen and they took ex-rays. The doctor said his leg was broken, and there was a fracture that had healed as well.

I was being accused of child abuse. I knew I hadn't hurt my son, but no one believed me. I'm sure my boyfriend had done this, but it was my word against his. I was never arrested, but was accused of child neglect for not protecting my son. He was taken to the hospital with double pneumonia and a broken leg that was healing on its own. I wasn't allowed to stay there. The welfare people gave custody of my son to my mother-in-law. I couldn't believe this was happening.

We had to go to court and the judge gave custody to my in-laws. Six months later we went back to court and nobody showed up. The judge said there was no one contesting and I could go get my son. When I went to get my son, his grandma was furious. She said she knew nothing about the hearing. I took my son and left.

The next thing I knew we went back to court, and I was given temporary custody for ninety days. The judge ordered me to go to counseling and not leave the county we lived in. I waited about six weeks and sent money to my friends that lived several counties away to rent me a house. We moved and no one knew where we were.

About two weeks went by and I started feeling bad for their grandma. I don't know why I did after all the things they had put me through. So I let my daughter call her grandma to let her know we were ok. That evening the police and the welfare people showed up to take my son away from me. It was heartbreaking for me not to be able to comfort my son. I'll never forget the way he looked as they drove off.

I told the police what had happened with me losing my husband before our son was born and that these people just wouldn't leave me alone to raise my son because they felt guilty about not knowing their own son, so they wanted my son to make things right for their loss. To me that's what I saw when it came to them. The police were very nice to me. They had seen my house and told me they would do anything for me to get my son back.

The next day I went to the office where my son was and tried to see him. They wouldn't let me. He cried most of the night, and it would upset him more if he saw me, so they took him back to his grandma's. I had to move back and establish resident. I had to go back to counseling as well.

Six months later we went back to court. This time they were trying to terminate my parental right all together because I had acted against the judge's ruling. They were certain that eventually I would give up, so they could take my son to raise as their own. The caseworker came to my house that morning and checked everything out and told me not to worry, that everything looked ok. When we went to court she was asked what she thought was best for my son. She said she didn't think he should be returned to me.

I still wasn't giving up. The grandma said they had two businesses and a stable home so my son would be well provided for. They never said anything about loving him. I was sure this time they thought I would break and let them have my son. But I wasn't about to give up!

When it was my turn to speak, I told the judge I was sorry for going against his past ruling. I told him I was trying to make a new life for my kids and me after losing my husband, and that these people were just trying to take my son to compensate for the loss of their son. Sure, they had money and it didn't matter how much it would cost, to take my son from me. I told the judge I was born poor and I would probably die poor, but I loved my son and I was having a hard time explaining to my daughter why her brother couldn't live with us. I told him I was doing the best I could with what I had to provide my kids with a good and stable home.

So the judge set another date to come back and allowed me to prove I was a fit mother. I asked the judge if I could have a new worker because I felt like the one that was assigned was being partial to the grandparents. He allowed my request. The next worker I got was someone I had grown up with and she knew what kind of life I lived growing up. We were very poor people and so was she. She would come to my house to make sure there was no drinking and that I was working steady trying to better myself for my kids. I started going to church and I got saved and was doing everything I was supposed to do.

Another six months passed, and I continued to go to counseling and stayed out of trouble. When we finally went back to court my worker was all for me getting my son back. She knew I had done everything that was required of me and my counselor had said the same thing. The judge said we would take a recess so he could make his decision. After what seemed like forever we went back to the courtroom. The judge ruled in my favor and I got my son. I had full custody of him, and it was worth everything I went through to get him back. I had finally proved myself. I never gave up.

BOLD IS BEAUTIFUL

AMY HALLER

Amy holds a degree in Health, Physical Education and Recreation from The University of Miami, and a Master's Degree in Education, specializing in Administration and Supervision from Augusta College. She also holds Coaching degrees in Life and Wellness Coaching, Positive Psychology, The Applied Neuroscience Institute as a Neuro Positive Trainer and is a Certified Performing Edge International Peak Performance Coach.

She is the founder of Inner Champion Coaching and specializes in motivating, educating, and communicating Peak Performance Skills and Strategies to her clients in both life and sport. She works with athletes, schools, teams, musicians, dancers and executives.

🏠 **www.innerchamps.com**

✉ **amy@innerchamps.com**

f **www.facebook/innerchamps**

🐦 **www.twitter.com/Amyhaller1**

in **Amy Haller – Inner Champion Coaching**

CHAPTER 4

A LIFE FILLED WITH GIVING AND RECEIVING

By Amy Haller

The Law of Giving and Receiving

"The universe operates through dynamic exchange... giving and receiving are different aspects of the flow of energy in the universe.

And in our willingness to give that which we seek, we keep the abundance of the universe circulating in our lives."

— *Deepak Chopra*

The Law of Giving and Receiving is the second law in Deepak Chopra's book, *The Seven Spiritual Laws of Success*. Every relationship is one of give and take, and the more you give, the more you will receive. The most important thing is the intention behind your giving and receiving. Giving is most effective when it is unconditional and from the heart. This is what I was given.

The most powerful forms of giving are non-material. Some of the most precious gifts you can give to others are the gifts of caring, affection, love, and appreciation.

This is why I have decided to tell my story based on The Law of Giving and Receiving. I was very fortunate to be the receiver of unconditional love and support from my parents and brothers. I grew up in a family where there was mutual respect, and a deep love between my parents. They treated each other so well, and were great role models for our family.

My dad was a very successful pediatrician and allergist, and his patients referred to him as Dr. Bob. He taught parent effectiveness training classes to the mothers in his practice. He provided his patients with the skills and knowledge to be effective parents. He was asked to teach sex education classes to kids in the school district. He gave so much to his profession, and in return, was loved by so many of his patients.

My mom worked as the bookkeeper for my dad's private practice. She was also very involved as a volunteer at the hospital, working in the surgical waiting room. She was so compassionate, and would comfort the families that were waiting for their loved ones while they were in surgery. She became the President of the Women's Board at the hospital and was also on the Ethics Committee. She was also very interested in English literature, focusing primarily on Dickens. She took courses for many years at The University of Buffalo. At the end of the course, she would invite the professor and the entire class over for a beautifully served lunch. She was a wonderful hostess and loved using her fine linens and silver for her guests. She was also a great conversationalist and enjoyed talking to people in all walks of life.

So here's the beginning of my story. When I was 9 years old, my parents signed me up for a summer tennis camp in a local park. I ended up winning the tournament at the end of the summer. As a result, I developed a real passion for tennis. I began taking lessons and competing in tournaments throughout the east coast. At 13 I was ranked #2 in the eastern section. My parents would travel with me to all the important tournaments regionally and nationally. I was building a very good reputation in Buffalo and on the east coast. I was the tennis playing kid pioneer from Buffalo, and progressed quickly with consistent publicity. It was at that point that my dad stopped playing golf and learned tennis. Not only did he love playing the game, but he also became a certified tennis umpire.

This was one of the important times when I realized how fortunate I was to be on the receiving end. I had parents that were extremely supportive, both with their time, and all the expenses that went along with it. I continued to compete until I was 18, and was awarded a tennis scholarship to The University of Miami. This was a big honor for me, and I know how proud my parents were. I spent the next 4 years competing on the tennis team at a high level, and received my undergraduate degree in Health, Physical Education, and Recreation. I proceeded to continue my education at Augusta College receiving a Master's Degree in Administration and Supervision. I was put on staff and was given a continuing education tennis class to teach at Augusta College. This was an invaluable experience for me, because I realized how much I loved working with people and teaching. They were large classes, and I thrived being in the role as their teacher.

After my master's degree, I decided it was time to move back north. I was offered a job as the first woman tennis pro at a club that was building a large program. This was one of the best decisions of my life! It was at my new job where I was introduced to my wonderful husband. He was working as a lawyer and would come to the club on the weekends to play tennis. Six months later we were engaged and have been happily married for the last 27 years.

My marriage has been a solid relationship based on mutual giving and receiving. Because I was given so much love as a child, I found it very natural to have the capacity to love my husband unconditionally. He was also raised in a loving family, and could therefore, genuinely give love to me. We were both very fortunate to grow up with parents that were so happy together. Experiencing this made it easier for us, and we learned so much from watching our parents.

A year after we were married, I was pregnant with our first child Katie. Two years later, Lucy was born. Our daughters are now 25 and 23. Having children was one of the most rewarding experiences of my life. They create a bond in a marriage that is so powerful. They are our focus and priority, and have added tremendous value to our lives. This is where the Law of Giving and Receiving comes into play. For me, being a mother is a continuation of the love that was given to me as a child. The circulation of life, the ability to give back to my daughters what was given to me. I feel extremely blessed to have my two loving daughters. They have given the love and respect to me that I gave to my parents.

In 2010 I became a Certified Life Coach (CPC). I proceeded to get degrees as a Neuro Positive Trainer, Positive Acorn Positive Psychology Coach, A New Life Story Wellness Coach, and a Performing Edge Coach. My hunger to keep learning stays with me each and every day. I have the experience, training, skills, and intuition to motivate and teach people how to be their best. This career path has tied together my past with my future, the circulation of life. I am continuing to grow my business and get involved in new and exciting areas. I find this work so rewarding and enjoy the opportunities of working with so many different people.

This past year has been very difficult for me because of all the losses I have had to endure. I have had to say goodbye to my adored 15-year-old miniature apricot poodle Kendall, my handsome 10-year-old black standard poodle Beau, but most importantly, my wonderful 87-year-old mother Mimi. Her death has made me cherish the mother-daughter relationship. I realize that nobody can ever fill her shoes (always Ferragamo!). It has been a life filled with unconditional love, support, and generosity. She gave so much as a mother, grandmother, and mother-in-law. I miss her presence so much every day, as well as the phone calls we had twice a day. She will always be in my heart, my role model, and one of my biggest fans. She loved hearing about my career as a life coach, and would always say how she wished Dad were still alive to see it.

I was devoted to her this past year as I watched her die of stage 4 lung cancer. I gave her back all the love and support that was given to me, the circulation of life.

Now it's my time to keep the cycle going, I will continue to give and receive in my personal life and career. The journey to live and love continues.

BOLD IS BEAUTIFUL

KATE GARDNER

Kate Gardner is an International Best Selling Author/Empowerment Coach & Video Creative Director who works closely with international best-selling authors and business owners to help them launch their books and products with video. Kate is also an empowerment coach who helps women become empowered and find their purpose. Kate is also the compiler of this amazing book project and the founder of the global campaign, The Freedom & Empowerment Campaign.

⌂ www.empoweringcoaching4women.com

⌂ www.successfulvideo.com

⌂ www.empoweringcoaching4women.com

⌂ www.successfulvideos.com

⌂ www.-the-missing-piece.com

⌂ www.freedomandempowerment.com

🐦 www.twitter.com/kategardner1979

f www.facebook.com/KIT1979

✉ kate@empoweringcoaching4women.com

CHAPTER 5

ON THE OTHER SIDE OF FEAR IS VICTORY

By Kate Gardner

That is a sentence that you hear me saying a lot, and will also hear my clients repeating daily to themselves after they have worked with me.

However, the truth is that 18 months ago on the other side of my victory was fear, and by the bucket load, I can tell you!

This is because 18 months ago I suffered from headaches and dizziness. At first I ignored them and just put it down to the stress of working full time, running my household and planning a wedding. But then the panic attacks would kick in, and I would find myself gripping hold of a trolley in the supermarket and using all my mental strength to keep my body upright and not fall over.

I visited the doctor, and he couldn't find any sign of anything wrong with me. He asked if I was under any stress, and I lied and said "no." He then gave me advice that I should have taken there and then. He said, "If you have something in your life at this present moment that is causing you stress, then do yourself the favor of cutting it out of your life before it makes you ill"(ding dong! Big sign to ditch your abusive partner there!). I did what every other victim of domestic violence does and carried on living in denial. I lied again to the doctor and said there was nothing wrong.

By now my home was no longer a home. As you well know, a home is where a person should feel relaxed and happy and contented, not be afraid of their partner or walking around on eggshells as not to upset him. My partner had a drinking problem, and it became worse to the point where the guy no longer knew what he was doing. Sinking 10-15 pints of Guinness a day had now become an everyday routine to him. He didn't care who he was hurting around him as long as he spent the afternoons in the pub, and abused me nightly.

Leaving the house early one morning to catch the bus into town, I was standing at the bus stop and I could feel a panic attack arising; my breathing became short and sharp, and it felt like the air didn't even fill a tiny corner of my lungs.

I boarded the bus and sat down to begin my journey, but suddenly blind spots appear in my eyes, which made me panic even more. It became a struggle to breathe properly. My head began to spin, and it took all my mental strength to try and stand up and walk along the bus aisle. I just managed to step off the bus.

I turned a street corner and propped myself up against a wall. Then pins and needles started to shoot from my shoulder down to my fingers and my arm became completely numb, I started to panic and cry. Oh god, what was happening to me? I had no control over my body and it was scaring me. The strangers in the street passed me and could see I was in an emotional state and tried to help.

It suddenly sprung to me that I had to get to the hospital, which was situated up the road from the center of town. I shoved my numb hand in my pocket and proceeded towards the hospital. God only knows how I managed that ten minute walk, but I did it. I walked through the reception doors of the hospital to be greeted by a male nurse. I told him that I thought I maybe having a funny reaction to something. He took me into a side room and told me to lie on a bed.

At that moment the right side of my body completely went numb, from my toes all the way up to the side of my head. I completely collapsed onto the bed and couldn't move. My tongue also went numb and the nurse kept asking me to calm down, but I couldn't. I had just lost control of the right side of my body, which is hardly something to be chilled and calm about!

The nurse hooked me up to a heart monitor; my heart rate was 125 beats per minute and increasing. The nurse stood to my left and repeated over and over, "Calm down. Please try to control your breathing, because if your heart rate goes any higher you will have to be rushed to the city hospital and you could go into cardiac arrest." I began to take control of my breathing and my heart rate began to drop slowly. However, my right side was still numb with painful pins and needles shooting up and down my body.

The nurse asked for my name, but when I tried to tell him but I couldn't say it. Instead it came out has a stutter "…Ka …Ka …Ka…" After three times I gave up, and tears fell from my face. I couldn't even do what we all take for granted every minute of every day; I couldn't talk, and I couldn't say my own name. The nurse rested his hand on my shoulder and said, "It's fine. I will let you rest for ten minutes and we will try again." I nodded my head as I wiped away my tears with the hand I could move.

I rested my head back on the pillow and began to realize full well why I was in that hospital bed, and what has caused me to be in that state. It was his doing, all of it was!

My partner arrived at the hospital 20 minutes later and came and sat beside me. All I could do was bore my eyes into him and feel a strong hatred against him. That's when it became clear to me that he will never change. A little voice came from deep inside and repeated itself over and over until it screamed in my head "LEAVE HIM!"

My head began to pound, and it felt like a train had crashed through my skull. A massive wave of tiredness also hit me and I felt sleepy. I closed my eyes because I didn't want to stare at the person who had caused me to be in this state. In fact, I wished him away there and then.

Two weeks later I received my test results. I had suffered a stroke and had scar tissue on my brain. This scar tissue was the cause of my paralysis. I was paralyzed for two months after that and could not move the right side of my body properly.

As soon as I could move my body again, I left my partner and moved six miles away to start my life over again; but unfortunately, four weeks into my new life I was hit again by more emotional trauma. I received a phone call one morning from the police to inform me my 14-year-old daughter had been raped. This completely devastated us. It left my poor child experiencing a nightmare, and left me, as her mother, a complete emotional wreck with zero self-confidence. My confidence was so miniscule that I feared even ringing for a take away pizza!

Fast forward 18 months to now, and I am an International Best Selling Author/Empowerment Coach & Video Creative Director who works everyday with International Best Selling Authors. I am also the founder of a global domestic violence campaign called The Freedom & Empowerment Campaign, which is known within 44 countries and comprises a team of 21 people across 7 countries. The campaign also includes Ambassadors who are #1 Best Selling Authors, and I am the compiler of a huge International Book Project called *The Missing Piece* that includes other amazing co-authors from all over the world.

The reason I wanted to share my success story with you is to let you know that my international success in the past 18 months was all built on facing huge fears. My legs would practically shake and my teeth would chatter when I first spoke on the radio, but over time facing these huge fears built my confidence into the person I am today.

In order to be successful in this world, there will be times when you are completely scared witless, and despite what you are feeling, you have to make bold movements in order to get to that other side. When you actually reach that other side it's there that victory lies, and so do many more amazing opportunities.

So I encourage you to make those bold movements and start making fear your best friend; start to live in that unknown zone and take risks, because on the other side of fear is victory!

I am living proof!

JASMIN CHRISTENSEN

Dr. Jasmin Christensen is the Founder of Healing Connections and Pathways. She started teaching and counseling while still on active duty in the USMC. She has accrued over 20 years of counseling and teaching experience. Empowerment and healing has been the main focus of her work with people across the US and on an international scale. She has lectured at various universities and colleges both nationally and internationally. She has the unique experience of working in trauma-related counseling, specifically trauma-related therapy onsite at disasters such as 9/11 in New York City and others. The idea of using Cognitive Behavioral Therapy has been something that Dr. Christensen has found useful with many clients. Using various healing techniques to help her clients overcome obstacles, move forward and become whole again is her main focus.

Helping people to heal themselves and their lives is her unique niche. Being an energy healer herself, she sees and feels first-hand what today's healers have to overcome and work past. Her unique connections with people, on a general basis, make her a popular and empathic counselor and Life Coach. Being a Multiple Sclerosis patient herself, Dr. Christensen has the first-hand experience of overcoming almost insurmountable odds just to achieve daily tasks. She has fully embraced her Wounded Healer Archetype and brings that experience to the table when assessing new clients and developing their individual programs.

- www.facebook.com/Healingconncections
- www.twitter.com/Greeneyedgoddes
- Author Page: www.jasminchristensen.wix.com/successbooks
- Website: www.healingconnectionsandpathways.com
- healingconnectionsandpathways@gmail.com

CHAPTER 6

$\mathscr{B}$E BOLD ENOUGH TO EMBRACE PEACE

By Dr. Jasmin Christensen

Bold, everyone talks about it. For years it had a duel meaning. "Bold" for men was a good thing, a heroic trait to have; for women, not so much. With phrases like "oh she's a bold one!" and "she's bold as brass," it was society's attempt to make sure that females were quiet, demure and obedient. In my opinion, if you want quiet, buy a doll! Pets are obedient, not people. Demure? That's an offshoot of the old adage, "children should be seen but not heard." Back in the days when girls were expected to sit quietly while their suitors looked them over and then made a deal with the girl's father for the purchase... errr, I mean marriage of the girl. She had no say in anything, not even the education and upbringing of her own children. Ah yes, those were the days. NOT!

I much prefer to remember those women of history that were bold as brass and accomplished a hell of a lot; in fact, they changed history. Every woman from Alfred the Great's daughter to Marie Curie and countless others in between, have been bold, determined and made some wonderful waves. Being bold is indeed a beautiful thing, hence the title of this book. We need to be bold if we want to see our dreams come true. In a world that will rip out your heart, stomp on it and kick it back in your face – yeah, we need to be bold.

Boldness isn't always about being brash and over the top; boldness is about being brave enough to step out of your fear and take those steps forward. When life has kicked you in the face and you feel so beaten down that giving up seems like the best option, be bold. Get back up

51

and stagger forward. When everyone else is telling you what to do and your heart is saying no, be bold. How do I know this? I didn't get to be 53 years old for nothing, and playing it safe was never in my nature.

But, in spite of the roughshod and rollicking adventuresome times, there were different types of challenges that came up. Sometimes life will surprise the hell out of you, and then you have to find a different way. When you're standing beside your child's grave and all you want to do is lay down beside it and let out the soul rending sobs that you've kept inside, do it. Be bold enough to let out the pain. If the people around you don't understand, to heck with them. There's nothing noble about keeping that much sorrow inside and letting it fester; it's insanity. When the sobs have subsided and you're lying there in the stillness, there is a sense of peace. Grab onto it. Let it fill your soul and your mind. There is a lot of strength in that peace. You'll need that strength to be able to stand up and walk back into life again.

We go through life at a fast pace, and the more energy we expend at pushing forward towards our goals, the better things go. Well, most of the time, not always. There are moments when that different type of boldness is again required. When you get that phone call from your father telling you that your only sibling has been killed, you have no choice but to rush home and be with your parents. Getting them through the sorrow and anguish of losing an adult child is not a task for the weak stomached.

That's the time for a different kind of boldness, the kind that is quiet but determined. The kind of boldness that is silent and caring, yet strong enough for everyone else to lean on. The kind of boldness that lets you get through being the first one at the mortuary to view your brother's body, to see if he viewable for your grieving parents. To look at the damaged face. He's barely recognizable, but he's there. You see glimmer of him around the reconstructive wax and funeral make up. You silently nod your head as the funeral director drones on about all the work they did and how proud they are of the end result. A silent boldness is present and you use it as your shield, your armor and your grounding point.

Because when it's over, and you finally have a moment where you don't have to take care of everyone else, you find yourself heading out to the loneliest spot you can think of. For me it was a nearby mountain, a tiny thing with trails going up it. I used to run up it a few years before when I was home on leave from the USMC. I parked my car and headed up the nearest trail. I ran every step of the way, ran every bit of anger, anguish and rage out of my system. When I reached the top, overlooking the river valley that my city rested in, I collapsed. In the cold Arkansas December drizzle at the top of that little mountain, I screamed and screamed and finally sobbed. Again, that moment of peace was right there before me. I clasped it close and found the strength to walk back down the mountain.

Life continues on and being bold carries us through most things, most situations and helps to define us. We all age, some gracefully and some not so much. As children grow up, it's a time to focus on those adventures that we couldn't take part in due to familial responsibilities. Me, I'm the type of bold that will hop on a plane and wind up 8,000 miles from home in the heart of India. Yeah, that was an amazing adventure. My husband and middle son had joined me for part of that journey, and we were amazed at the diversity of the country. We did loads of shopping and sightseeing, enjoyed the local cuisine, and just relaxed on a houseboat cruise along the backwaters of coastal southern India. I should have noticed then that my husband's health was not quite up to par, but when I asked him he just brushed it off with a "I'm just a little tired."

His being "just a little bit tired" turned out later to be a massive heart attack early one morning at home. It was right after Thanksgiving and the cardiologist definitely earned his fee that day. He came out to the waiting area where I was, and his face was pale; my heart lurched. He sat down beside me and said, "He made it, but just barely." The coming months were filled with more ER visits, more heart deterioration, and more tests. Finally, we were at a place where my husband of almost 23 years was succumbing to his genetics. A man who never smoked and drank rarely has a heart function of only 30%, and it won't improve but will continue to deteriorate. We are currently facing his receiving a defibrillator to keep his heart pumping when it does finally start to give out, as it surely will.

All of the boldness that had seen me through so many of life's events now had to take on a different role. I couldn't push my way through this, and I couldn't frenetically busy myself past any of it. Days, weeks, perhaps months are what we have. The idea of years is no longer an option. I've cried out my rage and anger over it all, and have found that in the face of this I have to embrace the peace once more. I can't go through his remaining days angry and full of rage; that isn't what I want for either of us.

So, I have found that in the boldness of my nature and my soul, I have found the courage to release the struggle and embrace the peace of the situation. After all, true free will is in play here and who am I to push against that? Loving someone means to respect their decisions, even if you don't agree with them. Embracing the peace means to let go of the end result, let go of all that we hang on to normally and simply embrace what is before us. Whether it's the death of a child, a sibling, or the impending death of a spouse and life partner, it is all filled with rage and anger. That only gets us so far, and then we have to be bold enough to embrace the peace that is before us. To not embrace it is to run the gauntlet of insanity and wind up in a black hole that few have ever crawled out of. So, be bold, grab onto that all that it entails for there is beauty in peace.

VERA SETTI MENEZES

As a psychologist, success coach and marketing expert, Vera feels a strong need for us, as women, to reclaim our feminine essence. She has been engaged in the movement to inspire women to reconnect with her feminine energy. Her joyful spirit shines through in her passion, commitment and devotion to serve as a catalyst on the unstoppable, crucial process of awakening our consciousness and feminine power. Her unique straightforward approach in a loving, compassionate way help her clients to ease through transitions and pains during this time of growth and co-creation, facilitating a path that brings the best of their selves to thrive and fulfill. By living both worlds, meaning sub-developed and developed countries, she has a broad vision of how women still have a long way to go, especially on a global scale.

As speaker, psychology teacher, group therapist and program developer for almost three decades, she has been part of multinational corporations such as Volkswagen of Brazil, Johnson & Johnson, White Martins and many others. Today, she has her own practice as a Success Coach, speaker, Host of many Interview Series and Program Developer to empower women to achieve personal and professional goals in a meaningful way.

🏠 www.verasettimenezes.com

🏠 www.globalfeminineshift.com

📞 (754) 367 0133

CHAPTER 7

HOW I SHIFTED FROM FIGHT, COMPETE AND CONTROL TO A STATE OF EASE, FLOW AND FORGIVENESS!

By Vera Setti Menezes

I grew up as a daughter of a military father who was my hero. I had three brothers and an older sister. My father was a dominant leader and my mother, despite being very competitive, lived submissive to my father's will, succumbing to the world of masculine energy. In those days in my country, it was accepted that men could do and have everything they wanted. I saw my father as unfailing, having all the admiration and respect from family and friends. I watched my three brothers have the freedom that I desired to have. This reinforced my painful and disadvantageous competition with my mother. That's why from an early age I started believing that the masculine way was the only one that would lead me to a successful life.

My relationship with my mother was always difficult, to say the least. The competition between us was very destructive. I was trapped in her powerful web of manipulation. I learned to master my competitive attitude surviving and co-existing in this environment. The unfair competition with my mother disempowered me, impeding my growth, self-expression and creativity. This was a big hindrance in the expansion of my true potential, never a fair game to play.

As a result I carried my competitive attitude beyond my mother, extending it into my relationship with my brothers, sister, friends and even men.

In regards to men, I entered relationships that were dominant and competitive, but at the same time, permissive and given to emotional abuse. In many instances, I took the financial responsibility, trading it for the last word. So it was during my first marriage. I believed I was in charge when, in reality, I was being manipulated by a dysfunctional and pathological person. Needless to say, after a short time it was over. I left the marriage a broken person. The only thing that made sense about this short-lived union was my daughter. Being a mother gave me a newfound taste for life.

Sadly, my unbalanced emotions caused me to move back with my parents. This only fueled my mother's anger against me. As my father took my daughter under his protection, her competition towards me became stronger. In consequence, I ended up losing the little bit of self-confidence I was building after the divorce. My parent's home was toxic. I had to get out from under my mother's control. In this quest for freedom and self-assurance, I only found loneliness. Men admired me, but could not stay with me. I was in and out of relationships, but competition and control issues always got the best of me. I remained a single mother for 18 years. I then met a new person and remarried. However, I still wasn't ready to share my true self with someone.

This became clear when my second husband couldn't accept my controlling and territorial disputes anymore. Over financial crises, in which we lost everything, we ended up divorcing after five years of marriage. It was the most crucial and painful moment of my life, and yet it was a starting point for my extraordinary transformational journey.

I was frustrated, lonely, unhappy and in financial despair. My life seemed to have no more meaning. My only daughter, whom I always cared for, was now married and taking care of her own family. I could no longer hide behind my workaholic mask. My career as a fashion designer lost its appeal to me. Going back to my practice as a psychologist would take too long to establish. This lack of vision and motivation, made me try several career paths only to fail over and over again.

In the midst of everything, I realized how much I was out of balance with myself and the world around me. The masculine force that drove my life had become destructive. Adrenaline levels were increasing my stress. I had become my worst enemy.

I started to question myself, to ask why all these things were happing to me, why I was lonely and unhappy. Why men admired me, but couldn't stay with me for good. Why I needed to have so many people under my control just to receive emotional and financial support. My masculine model of operation was supposed to bring me everything, and I ended up with nothing!

After many sleepless nights and days of deep emotional pain, I finally start to soften up from the inside out, letting go of my frustration, anger, disappointment and fear. I started allowing my heart to speak, and, at the same time, I started listening to my intuition. And from the deepest of my soul, I started listening to the call of my inner voice asking for a new me to emerge.

I came to the realization that there isn't a quick fix. I allowed myself to go through a long process of transformation. And for the first time, I let go of the masculine model I was trapped in, understanding that it wasn't the best for me. I allowed myself to accept that I was vulnerable and that it was OK to show my weakness. And only then I could reach out for help. Only then did I become open to receive the help I needed, but I was too proud to admit. So empowered by this new realization, I picked up my pieces and put myself together, nurturing a vision of a better life.

I pursued a new career as a Success Coach sharing my experience with others and enabling them to look beyond their issues. I engaged in different programs and studied all that I could in a short period of time. During this process I totally changed my old paradigms. When I was feeling weak, in reality, I was getting stronger by growing my consciousness and by embodying my inner power. I found my true self and became the most authentic me I had ever been. Looking from the inside out, I found within me new talents and opened up my whole being for new possibilities.

After one year of intense inner work, a great sense of serenity began to shower over me. What once had never blossomed started to flourish. So it happened that from within a deep soul connection, I embraced my true feminine essence. On that very moment my life began to make sense.

I realized that all the disagreement between my mother and me sprang from own inner battles, from her sense of loss and lack of freedom, not mine. I also realized that I would never satisfy her desires or her dreams. She would have to do it on her own. All I can do for her is to offer her my understanding and support, while not allowing her to control me by her fears or frustrations.

This was my awakening. Acceptance and forgiveness were the bandages that would bind the wounds that resulted from years of a painful relationship between us. I finally could understand that my mother's role in my life was to help my soul expand. From it, I have learned how to forgive and even bless her soul. Her mission, I assume, was to give birth to someone that one day would be inspiring to other women and lead them to embrace their own femininity. By doing so, they will find their true purpose in life and continue a transformational cycle by benefiting others from their own experience.

I feel blessed to have had this opportunity to learn and grow from this very exhaustive and painful experience of mine. I am glad I could go beyond my five senses as a human being in this realm to fully understand my non-physical dimension There I learned that feelings of rejection, pain, frustration and competition allied with years of trying to fix others, trying to get attention, and being self-centered and anxious gave the wrong kind of power to my ego. I learned that acceptance, forgiveness, refraining from judgment, love, detachment and trust come from the nonphysical part of me. I accepted that I came into this world to experience this realm.

My intention is to use what I perceived from this contrast and offer it up to empower mother and daughter relationships. I believe if they understand who they really are and what roles they have in this world, their relationship will be the most profound and meaningful – a transformational experience, more than any other they could ever have. Mothers and daughters can share in a beautiful relationship even if it is challenging and painful at times. You may never fully comprehend all its peculiarities and delicate nuances, but you will learn to love and accept one another as women who are connected by their feminine essence just like it is supposed to be.

Today I'm able to listen to my heart and let my deepest desires come out without judgment. I'm humble and vulnerable in the most positive meaning of the words. I found my true purpose in life, and for the first time I have a feeling of profound joy and fulfillment. I don't have any need to compete between my two forces, which I define as the masculine and feminine energies. I embrace both, and I live in a state of ease and flow. I found my balance. Now I'm ready to give and receive love!

BELLE KOHEN

Belle Kohen has lived an interesting life to date. Currently, she is the CEO of Creative Coaching LLC as a Life, Business, and Accountability Coach with certification from Coach U. Having worked in many diversified professions spanning decades, Belle's careers have included: Registered Dental Hygienist, Dental Practice Management Consultant for 1-800 Dentist and Mercer Advisors. She also owned and operated a Petland franchise, is a self-taught screen printer, and an advertising specialties guru. She is currently a property manager for L&F Investments LLC, a family owned business. She has been married nearly 40 years, has two children and four grandchildren. Always willing to help way beyond the norm, Belle has found her niche as a Coach. For her, it is a way to help others while immensely enriching her own life

✉ **coachbelle@gmail.com or bellekohen@sbcglobal.net**

📞 **(248) 765 0353**

Ⓢ **Skype: Belle Kohen**

🏠 **www.coachbelle.com**

f **www.facebook.com/CreativeCoachingllc**

f **bellekohen@facebook.com**

in **www.linkedin.com/pub/belle-kohen/10/910/84**

𝕏 **www.twitter.com/bellekohen**

 www.pinterest.com/bellekohen

Oakbrook Terrace, Illinois and Bloomfield Hills, Michigan

CHAPTER 8

HOW TO PLAN FOR AN EXTRAORDINARY LIFE

By Belle Kohen

I am not a television viewer; however, I did see an interesting program once about how incredible it is that humans exist. The actual process of the cells dividing and multiplying correctly and eventually leading to a healthy, viable person is a miracle. Most of us have the ability to think, plan and carry out what could be an extraordinary life. I feel that I have accomplished many things in my life; yet, I am always open to the possibilities of what else I can do to make my life better and make a difference in other peoples' lives.

Many of my life experiences relate back to my childhood and the fact that I am a middle child. Middle kids are at times responsible for their younger siblings, and that is where I believe all my nurturing, caring and compassion come from. This phenomenon carried through into adulthood in a powerful way. In fact, there are times when I have gone above and beyond what a sibling, parent, or any person should do! I have more recently learned many lessons about setting boundaries, taking care of myself and growing as an individual.

These lessons showed me the importance of living in the present and paying closer attention to those around me. I learned an enormous amount from my experiences and would like to share some of the trials and tribulations of being a life coach and entrepreneur.

I have been married to the same man for nearly 40 years. I have two adult children. Their spouses are great matches, wonderful people, and they are in love. They each have two children, who are the greatest joy in my life. Both families are able to manage their own households without any parental help or intervention. I am flattered when they ask a question or for an opinion. I am continually learning to keep my thoughts to myself and to let them raise their children and run their households as they please. I already had my chance, and I could not be prouder of the people they have become.

I spent roughly thirty years as a hygienist and consultant in the dental field. I see clearly that what I have to offer as a coach is easily carried over to any profession. It is always about listening carefully to my clients and allowing them the time to set and reach their goals, whatever they may be.

As a coach, I feel extremely passionate about what I do, as I see the changes that my clients have made in their lives. Some need coaching around an idea for a business. Others may need the nuts and bolts of how to set a business up from scratch. At times, I switch hats from coach to mentor to knowing that teaching the elementary steps of Business 101 will move my clients forward with much less frustration than the slow and tedious process of learning it by themselves. For this, they are extremely grateful. There are some clients who think and process information differently than I do. For those, there are classes available to teach the entire business process in order to work out their own plan. We all learn differently and I respect that. There are even some who have no idea what they want. They haven't taken the time to thoroughly think about it. There are people in our history, like Albert Einstein, Bill Gates and Steve Jobs, who tried different endeavors without worrying about failure. They had to try more than once to finally achieve their dreams. A red light should not stop your trip from ultimately reaching the final destination. I often suggest that clients pretend they are a child again and dream with no restrictions.

There is much talk today about thinking outside the box, and yet, so many people are unable to. This is heartbreaking, because we as human beings have the capacity to be anything we want and achieve almost anything we dream of. It is more a matter of thinking, planning and executing those dreams.

Just recently, my father-in-law passed away. The impact on our family continues to be devastating; yet, the outpouring of contributions, notes and letters about him is amazing. He was a very special man in many ways. My goal in telling his story is not only from my perspective as a coach, but also to point out how much we take our lives for granted. I have learned a great many lessons from my father-in-law, Zoli. Many of his qualities are so significant that perhaps we should ask ourselves to use some of them every single day and teach others to use them as well.

He was a religious man.

He was a quiet man, or, shall I say, a man of very few words most of the time.

He had a few true friends, but not many.

He never dwelled on things, instead, he thought them through, and let them go.

He always listened very carefully, and was thoughtful and truthful with his answers.

He was sincere, honest, and genuine. He was also extremely patient and deliberate.

He changed jobs and professions many times in his lifetime without fear or anxiety.

He always put himself in others' shoes in order to see situations from a different perspective.

He always had nice things to say about others; otherwise, he said nothing at all.

He never spoke unkind words behind anyone's back.

He was a rich man, not in dollars, but in his love for his family.

His family was his greatest inspiration. That was what he lived for.

His family kept him going until his last breath by prodding him to eat a little more, drink another sip of water, say a few more words, or stay awake just a little later in the evenings.

He always helped others without hesitation, expecting nothing in return.

The number of years he went to school didn't matter, because he learned life by living it.

He was a survivor of the Holocaust, and rarely spoke about his experiences.

When asked his opinion about a situation, whether it was politics, clothing styles, or religion, he would always think before he spoke and answer carefully.

These are very admirable qualities in a human being. I ask myself repeatedly how many of them I will follow regularly. My lessons from his life are to have more patience, not to judge others, to listen more carefully, be more tolerant, not to dwell on things, choose my friends with care, and look at the situations from another's perspective rather than just my own.

We need to remember that we are only on this planet for a finite amount of time, and that every day must have some joy, fun and happiness in it. This is a lesson well learned on how to lead an extraordinary life.

CHRISTINE CATOGGIO

Speaker

Senior Issues

Educator

Senior Care Coordinator

Life Transition Coach

Founder of "Successful Life Transitions"

Life & Family Transition Specialist

Known as the Life Navigator and Guide Through Unchartered Life Change, Christine is passionate about helping men and women understand and navigate the many challenges of life transitions. Christine inspires and motivates business owners and entrepreneurs to survive and thrive through the processes of change and transition in their own lives.

Christine maintains an active Care Management Practice, and coaches individuals and families as they deal with the transitions of Aging parents, while experiencing their own issues. Christine understands first-hand the challenges that adult children of aging parents face, and is passionate about helping families share long healthy lives and strong relationships with peace of mind and quality of life.

Christine is a Life Transition specialist, and her services and programs have helped many clients locally and globally.

Christine holds a number of industry certifications, and in 2008, was named Soroptimist of Boca Raton Woman of Distinction for her charitable work to the community and as Assistant Governor of the four Boca Raton Rotary Clubs, Christine is a Past Secretary, Past President, Current Board Member & Member of Boca Sunset Rotary Club.

For more information on Christine or to schedule her for speaking presentations, please visit her at www.christinecatoggio.com or email her at ccatoggio@msn.com.

📞 **(561) 929-1195**

📞 **(888) 561-AIPS (2477)**

🏠 **www.christinecatoggio.com**

f **www.facebook.com/christine.catoggio**

in **www.linkedin.com/in/ccatoggio**

CHAPTER 9

EMPOWERING CHANGE: ALL ENDINGS HAVE NEW BEGINNINGS!

By Christine Catoggio

When a playwright is telling a story and wants to change the theme but continue the story, he calls it Act II or Second Act.

When a musical group wants to re-ignite or re-introduce their once popular band, they call it a revival.

As I pondered what would be the best way to tell my story, I determined it should be "Second Act—The Revival"! The Life Story continues, in a new and exciting way.

"I was raised to sense what someone wanted me to be and be that kind of person. It took me a long time not to judge myself through someone else's eyes."

– Sally Field

Growing up I learned at a young age to strive for perfection. 100% on an exam was greeted with "Why not 105?"

It was playful, and somewhat congratulatory, but it set a standard for myself that was difficult to sustain. I created this expectation for myself, this level of perfection, of always trying harder, always being the perfect little girl that everyone wanted and expected me to be. I was

69

"the good one." The one who never got into trouble and always based my actions and decisions on those expectations. I always followed the rules and never allowed myself to color outside the lines, because I knew that was not allowed and totally unacceptable. What a difficult standard I created for myself!

So, at almost 50 years old, as life as I knew it began to crumble, so did my yen for perfection.

If I never broke the rules, and all the rules around me are now changing, then how do the "rules" fit my life? — they no longer pertain.

But, my life was in such disarray, how was I to know what was right or wrong anymore? What is the norm? Which direction do I follow?

Confused, bewildered, and totally broken, I didn't recognize this life of mine. It was not the life I had intended for myself. Everything was different. Nothing was the same. Everything had changed. The only constant, my AHA, was CHANGE!

Suddenly, I realized, that I needed to be friends with change, because it was the only thing that I could count on.

Life has a way of showing us direction, pointing us where we are meant to go. There is a commercial on TV that uses that premise: "Follow the green arrow—we'll show you how to handle all your finances." My fascination has always been "Follow the Yellow Brick Road." As in the case of Dorothy (from the Wizard of Oz), the yellow brick road did show her which way she needed to go. The path was all laid out for her. She just needed to follow the road to find what she was looking for. But, just like Dorothy, we get distracted along the way. We lose sight of the goal, or, in many cases, never really know what we want to begin with! Those bright shiny objects will get us every time. We fall in love, have kids, and want the perfect fairy tale life. We get so caught up in the "we want it now" mode that we fail to see the path that is laid out before us.

As the rules of my life changed, I began to notice the path that I had ignored. But part of me wanted to stay in ACT I. It was comfortable, it was me (so I thought), it was what I was accustomed to. It was "life according to Christine." It was the life that society, family, and an Italian Catholic upbringing told me to be!

But, slowly, surely, the curtain came down on ACT I and there was nothing but darkness.

"In search of my lost innocence I walked out a door. At the time I believed I was looking for a purpose, but I found instead, the meaning of choice."

– Liv Ullmann

ACT II

The dark can be a scary place. Not being able to see what lies in front of you, but totally immersed, drowning, in a sea of emotions is frightening.

As I look back on some early journal entries, "so much pain. I want more than anything for this heartache to be over." Like a loved one dying of cancer, you want it to end. Even though the end may not be easy or painless, you want the suffering to end. The anticipation, the not knowing and the unforeseen, is a slow death.

Then slowly, the curtain starts to rise on Act II and a new perspective starts to emerge. I remember acknowledging the pain, but becoming more determined than ever to fight through it. An overwhelming sense of survival took over and "flight becomes fight."

Even though I did not recognize this life anymore, I began to capture remnants of my former life, my former self and intertwine them with new discoveries, new perspectives and a release of the old. And suddenly, unexpectedly a beautiful mosaic started to unfold right before my eyes.

I found new interests and new passions, and a new perspective on the road that I was facing. And, the more I focused on the new possibilities, new opportunities started to present themselves. And, I found that I was becoming more accepting of a new path and started to embrace the prospective path that was developing right before my eyes. And,

71

the more accepting I became, the more determined I became to survive, thrive and create a life of purpose and fulfillment.

"Class is an aura of confidence that is being sure without being cocky. Class has nothing to do with money. Class never runs scared. It is self-discipline and self-knowledge. It is sure-footedness that comes with having proved you can meet life."

– Ann Landers

Wow! I was becoming one "Classy" lady!

Determination and confidence are the result of painstakingly having met the challenges that life presents and surviving. And surviving with heart, soul and dignity in tact—that's thriving!

Change is empowering. Facing fears and coming out the other side is not only Bold—it is Beautiful! It teaches us things about ourselves we never knew. I learned qualities and strengths that I never knew existed. It offers the opportunity for new choices and new beginnings.

When I look back on my ACT I, I barely recognize that person.

ACT II is a woman of confidence, self-assuredness and content with who I've become. I am not afraid of getting lost because I know that I will always find my way back. And I am not afraid of being alone, for that is when I find out who I truly am.

LEXIS JOHNSON

Three decades in the making, MuffinTopDiet.com was created by a woman who melts stress. Award winning Lexis Johnson, PhD learned alternative healing modalities of color therapy, nutrition, emotional heart resonance, psychology, aromatherapy, meridian therapy and over 20 different types of energy work like Reiki. Working with the physical, emotional, mental and spiritual, Dr. Lexis found solutions to the stress that causes or contributes to most illnesses. Check out Muffin Top Diet in the iTunes store.

⌂ www.MuffinTopDiet.com

⌂ www.WinAtLosingDiets.com

⌂ www.thePrettyWomanWebsite.com

CHAPTER 10

TURN YOUR SNEAKY, SCARY, SORROWFUL STRESS INTO SEXY, SLEEK, SUCCULENT SUCCESS!

By Lexis Johnson

Men! My man! His idea of creating a business was like the Lone Wolf in the pack. Me? Well, he thought I could never do it. But I showed him, not because I was out to show him or anyone else anything, but because I had to. Women everywhere must see that they can do it too. I became a leader to show them the way. My story wasn't easy but it brought me to myself.

Writhing on the floor in the worst pain I'd ever felt. Was it my stomach or my lungs? Worse than childbirth. No one would help me, or believe me! Seven months pregnant - this was definitely not labor. Hubby at the table eating breakfast I'd prepared. While eating a banana, suddenly my world collapsed! Like thunderbolts, the pain seared through my insides until tears rolled down my cheeks. Why wasn't he moving to help me?

A controlling man, he thought I was pretending to gain sympathy, trying to get him to stay home instead of going away on yet another business trip. I had little kids at home, and it would be great if he'd spend some time with us. But that's another story.

Throat closing up… couldn't breathe! Gasping I begged "hospital!"

"Well, Lexis," my doctor said, "you had an allergic reaction to a banana. Because of it we discovered you're a Celiac, have an ulcer, pleurisy on your lungs and an embolism, a blood clot on your lung. You're lucky you aren't dead!"

"Great! Let's just add that to the fibromyalgia and Crohn's the specialist diagnosed last year! What do we do about it?"

"Not much we can do. Virtually everything we could do would initiate premature labor or is contra-indicated during pregnancy. Demerol will ease the pain. You can go home in a few days, but no more bananas and stop stressing."

Flat on my back, and the kids needing me at home; one unborn and I'm floating on the ceiling high on Demerol! Can't be good for the baby... It gave me time to think about having been a sickly kid. My mom fed me homemade soups and juices that she had made in a juicer. I got better. I married a meat-and-potatoes man and got sicker. I was helping him create his million dollar business, but it wasn't mine. It wasn't what I wanted to do. He didn't appreciate my help or my needs. Hmmmm...?

With the hubby away I thought about all my health troubles. I thought I had it figured out when I learned I had Candida, not the vaginal kind but the systemic kind. I went on an anti-Candida diet to control the overgrowth and felt better. Then the problems came back differently. What about food allergies? But a rotation diet made me sensitive to everything I ate!

Doing this on my own was clearly not working. I went to a 21st century allergy specialist who reduced my diet to just turkey, cantaloupe, broccoli and cauliflower for a month! By the next visit I had been successfully de-sensitized from a whole bunch of foods that I could now eat again. Phew! What a difference, but I was still exhausted. My husband thought I was a hypochondriac, just wanting his attention. He was too busy building a business to worry about me...

I tried diets to improve digestion and added soy. Big mistake! Soy depresses thyroid function and disrupts hormones. Next! I tried various diets, adding and subtracting this food, that supplement, fine-tuning what I knew. I eventually discovered what worked for me. There was such a difference in me and my kids that my friends and my kids' friends' moms wanted my secret. Why had there been such a dramatic turnaround in my hyperactive kids? Why was I glowing in good health when months before I was sullen, gray, moody, exhausted, weak, covered in rashes, hives and acne with greasy hair? My whole family had improved!

Long ago I left my controlling husband. I was free to pursue what I wanted to do. I had helped so many women and their kids that I decided to get my credentials and do what hubby never allowed me to believe was possible – I started my own business!

I'd figured out that there wasn't just one thing wrong with all these women. Every one of them had different combinations of the same things askew. Physical, mental, emotional, spiritual. Many of them said their kids were getting fat, they themselves had belly fat, junk in the trunk, love handles, and on and on. Their symptoms were headaches, recurring colds and exhaustion – all kinds of similar problems to mine.

As decades went by, each generation of women had new names for the same thing. Slogging it out at the gym gave them skinny legs and arms, but they still had that spare tire around the middle! We looked like muffins with last years' jeans fitting except for spillage of excess over the top of those jeans. Women started calling this the "muffin top."

Most of these women said they were not feeling heard by their doctors or anyone. Doctors prescribed tranquilizers, drugs like Prozac, to shut them up. Others told them it was all in their heads, to grow up, stop whining. We weren't whining, but we also weren't being heard. When others wouldn't listen to these women, I decided I'd listen. I'd be there for them. I'd help.

I've led a very stressful life. I left my husband when my seventh baby wasn't even two. I packed up and got out! It took me seven years to finally get a divorce because he had money and because he could. He thought I couldn't live without him. I know he felt I needed his money to get by. He was abusive; he had gotten physical with me and one of my children, and I wasn't going to take it anymore. I was never going back no matter what.

I felt as though I'd never make it in this new world of single working parents. So I started studying and got myself educated in every possible way I could think of. I needed answers to know how to help these women, my kids and myself.

I became a licensed aesthetician with a focus on the body, a registered aromatherapist, and studied three different schools of nutrition. Each modality taught me more about the body: color and sound therapy, Reiki, eventually becoming Master of over 20 different types of energy healing. I studied all the greats in holistic and alternative healing and psychology. I'll always be learning. I want to be the voice for women everywhere.

Having been brought up in a family business, I wanted to own my own business like my parents and husband had. I wanted it to be mine so no one would ever have control over me again. I wanted to use the information I had gleaned through all my struggles – through taking care of my aging mom until her death, raising my seven kids alone, and through my second marriage to my very best friend of 36 years only to have him pass away in his sleep after only six and a half years of marriage. My heart felt ripped out!

Yes. I know. Stress – and that was it! Stress was the answer to all my queries after three decades of working on myself and others. Common themes were found when I looked at emotional, mental and spiritual causes too. My solutions were found!

I created Questionnaires to hear what the body's symptoms were screaming out; Questionnaires that deciphered the body's many cries for help and a System I could individualize that would help each and every woman who came to me. It works!

My business was born through trial and error, case study after case study, stress upon stress until I finally figured it out. Muffin Top Diet was born: a system, a program, and a series of questionnaires to individualize each woman's problems based on her symptoms and stressors. It worked for everyone who tried it.

Without the support of my husband, my brothers, my parents or any other man, I worked diligently and together with each of the women in my case studies until I fine-tuned a system that works every time for everyone.

Stress aggravated and caused all the problems that I had and that each of them had. I put my system online in Kindle books, a magazine and a program all called Muffin Top Diet, so that I could help millions of women.

Men build businesses like they hunt: either as lone wolves or in packs. Women find safety in numbers just like we did in cave man days! Because of all the wonderful women I have worked with, I am thriving today. I am healthy. I am self-supporting, self-sufficient and very gratified with the work I created, that I love, and the warmth I get from all the women I help. Today I am Bold and Beautiful with my own business MuffinTopDiet.com.

ANGELA PENNY

Angela Penny is a dreamer at heart and an entrepreneur to the core. Her happiness comes from creating, whether it's a painting, writing a story, planning a new business or testing a recipe; she is most content when she can make something where there was once nothing.

She lives out loud, finds beauty in unexpected places, encourages others to follow their hearts, and belly laughs every single day.

She lives on a mountain in beautiful Cape Breton Island in Canada with her husband Ryan, three children Jayce, Charlie, and Ty, and a few dozen feathered and furry companions.

✉ angela@cabrestoridge.com

CHAPTER II

*O*FF TRACK

By Angela Penny

Perhaps this is a story about friendship, or healing, or two lost souls who found in each other what they were missing in the world. I don't know how to label this relationship, but I know it's real. I know that because, as a result of it, I discovered how to be fearless and follow my heart to a passionate life that I had once thought was only available in my dreams.

Maybe being bold isn't about winning awards or achieving sales and recognition in business. Maybe being bold happens when you walk away from everything that you once thought you wanted, even if it shifts your entire world upside down. At least that's how it happened for me.

I can still remember the day I changed my mind. I was sitting in an office chair while I rattled off forecasted numbers and revenue projections trying to figure out exactly what I needed to do to launch my business into the next realm. I had met a buyer who liked my products and the potential deal had the possibility of changing my entire life. This is what I wanted, right? I wanted success measured in sales, right? When I was asked that day, "So, what do *you* want?" I suppose my reply was meant to be relevant to the discussion, but from the depths of my heart came an answer that I had no control over, I blurted it out without that half-second pause that normally filters those things that should remain unsaid.

"Horses" I answered.

Yes, yes, I would get them, *eventually*, I was told, I just had to stay focused. Give it another 5 or 10 years, grow and sell the business, and then I'd have plenty of time for horses.

Another 5 or 10 years? Was this supposed to appease me? Should it have seemed like an insignificant measurement of time? It didn't. It felt like it could have been an eternity. I had already put my love of horses on hold when it was apparent that the financial strain of being a teenage mother could not afford both diapers and riding lessons. Then another baby in my early twenties, a young marriage, saving for a house and life and businesses, all kept the pause button down for longer than I had ever anticipated.

My entire soul ached for a horse. Unless you have ever had that connection with a big beautiful animal yourself, my words cannot aptly give justice to the longing in my heart. I had never owned my own, but was lucky enough to grow up riding other people's horses, trusting that someday I would have a horse just for me. We had recently bought a new home with plenty of acreage, but now it felt like this dream was slipping further and further out of my reach.

That was the day it ended for me. The creativity for the business, the addiction to the success and chasing deals, it was all dead to me. I left that meeting feeling like my entire life was on the wrong track. This business was supposed to bring me closer to my dreams, not keep them at bay. I decided, driving home, that I wasn't going to do it anymore. I was closing my business.

When I walked away from what I had created, I felt like the bottom had dropped out of my life. I was depressed, lonely, and unattached to any reason to get dressed or remain out of bed for extended periods of time. I was stuck in transition. There were days that I was sure that I would give up these horrible feelings of discomfort for the busy life that I had once complained about, the chance to go back to the way it was. It was terrible knowing that I had made this choice, yet it left me feeling so broken. I was unsure why I didn't stay there. People go to jobs every single day that they don't feel passionate about, why couldn't I have done that too? Why did I have to disappoint the people who believed in me and in my business? It was a dark period of my life, stuck in limbo, my faith was wavering, and I had no idea how I was supposed to get out of the mess I had created. I also had no way to understand yet that my life had shifted in agonizing ways to allow room for what I was supposed to attract, for what was meant to happen.

I had always pictured my first horse as being a beautiful steed. I had visions of shopping for him, of competing with him, and about the kindred bond that we would share. I had thought about him for my entire life, and I was confident that I knew what I was looking for. Imagine my disappointment when my husband agreed to bring home a horse that was the complete opposite of what I had waited for my entire life. This was a horse I knew and disliked because of his ornery disposition and complete lack of respect for people in general. A racehorse that was forced off the track and into retirement because of an injury was definitely not what I had dreamed about, but my husband knew that we were his last chance; if a home wasn't found for him he would be shipped to slaughter.

I remember the day he arrived at the barn close to our home where we were going to board him. I could hear him hollering before the truck and trailer pulled into the yard, and when the trailer door opened, he backed off like a bolt of lightning. He was large, strong, disrespectful, and unfortunately, *mine*. How was I going to get myself out of this? We could afford one horse, and he was it.

I can tell you for the first month that I had him, he scared me. I didn't want him, but I found myself with him throughout the day regardless. I had to take care of him, because I was all he had; so those first weeks, there was no love, only pity. Pity for this animal who was supposed to be killed, but somehow ended up in my care. I dreaded going to see him, but I did it anyway. I got myself out of bed and dressed, and would spend time with him. Brushing him while dodging threatening bites, feeding him while dancing around threatened kicks, and crying myself to sleep at night wondering how I was going to fix him.

Someone said to me that his behavior was dangerous, and it was my responsibility to change it before he hurt someone. That was the day I made up my mind to take control, to handle my fear and teach this horse some manners. I read everything I could get my hands on, watched hours of training videos, and asked anybody who would lend me their ear for a moment to share their thoughts on changing his behavior. Anything new that I learned I would test it on him. I was learning so much that I had to spend hours working with him every day. Eventually, I got to learn where he liked to be touched, and the spots that a touch made him nervous. I learned how to feel calmer around him, and how, at the very moment I would relax, so would he. He was so in tune with my emotions that if I wanted to work with him, I had to let go of any anxiety and expectations in order for our time to be productive.

Soon, I couldn't wait to get to the barn. I couldn't wait to spend time with him, try new things with him, or sit quietly next to him while he grazed in the pasture. I started telling him things that I wasn't comfortable telling anyone else. I shared my hopes, my fears, my dreams and my regrets with him. The horse that didn't like to be cuddled allowed me to cry into his mane when I couldn't hold it in any more. He'd nicker softly when he'd see me coming. He became soft and trusting, and learned how to bow politely for a carrot. We managed to create a relationship unlike anything I'd ever experienced.

I give credit to him for not only making me get out of bed and out of my funk, but in reminding me that I feel so much passion for horses that it was my true calling to create a life of being surrounded by these majestic animals. My husband and I purchased the riding stable where we boarded him, and I now spend my days immersed in a horse world, teaching lessons, and loving life.

His name is RH Rambler.

He is my horse, and I am his girl.

I know that I saved him from an early death, but he gave me permission to be alive again, which is remarkably the same thing.

BOLD IS BEAUTIFUL

LINDA DRAKE

As the founder of Trailblazer Advisors, Linda Drake deploys transformational breakthrough technologies, Leadership Success Journeys, to enable individuals attain the highest levels of success and satisfaction in their personal and professional lives.

Previously, Linda was the founder and chair of a global information services company providing customer support outsourcing for the Fortune 50 and an honored recipient of numerous national, state and local awards.

Contact us about Leadership Success Journeys...

Where the only journey that matters is yours!

✉ **Linda.Drake@TrailblazerAdvisors.com**

⌂ **www.TrailblazerAdvisors.com**

f **www.facebook.com/ Linda Drake**

in **www.linkedin.com/in/lindadrake**

🐦 **www.twitter.com/linda_drake**

CHAPTER 12

SOMETIMES WE DECIDE TO CONTRIBUTE TO THE WORLD FOR PURELY ALTRUISTIC REASONS: THIS IS MY SOMETIME.

By Linda Drake

Sometimes the Divine intervenes like a laser beam directing the way: This was God's sometime.

I was living outside of Philadelphia; it was the end of a good year and I had planned a themed Christmas party for my friends and their spouses. I always had a theme, and we always had so much fun. I believe that was the year of the Christmas Costume Pajama Party; friends and couples were so very clever. Half the fun was seeing how people interpreted the theme.

And the strangest thing is that I had learned about discount tickets for a great play in New York City just weeks before and was able to get those tickets (and great seats) for a Saturday night in early March. I bought four tickets, and I had in mind to invite three of my dear female friends the night of the Christmas party. Know that these were my friends; at the start, they were not close friends with one another.

Before the night's end, I called these friends together in the hall away from the crowd and announced, "I have tickets!" Little did I know that these three simple words would lead to an adventure of a lifetime!

So there we were in March in a rented limousine for a weekend in New York City. Somehow, my intuition told me this trip would be majestic! The chemistry and energy of this group of four were unbelievably magnetic! We laughed all the way there, through the play and all weekend long. One of us suggested that we name the newly formed association. It only took moments as we looked among ourselves, (because at our stage in life, we all needed glasses to read and we all should have chains around our necks for easy access to our "opticals") and with a simple idea and a tacky, totem gift a friendship clique was born – The Chick Chain Court!

But by the end of the weekend, these pillars-of-the-community, middle-aged women were laughing like schoolgirls. And as we deepened the imagery and the bond, we projected ourselves as members of the "Court", fantasy royalty, and we created names for each other. After all, what is a Court without titles? There was Lady Jester, the Duchess, the one and only Principessa, and yours truly, tq (yes, small "tq" for the queen, just another servant of the Court!). What a weekend! What a month.

It was 4:11 PM on the last Friday in March when my phone rang. "Mrs. Drake?" "Yes," I responded. "This is Dr. M. Your breast biopsy has tested positively for cancer. Make an appointment with my office next week." Silence.

The earth moved. And so did the Court. My friends and our magical connection came to my psychic rescue.

It was not long after absorbing the news that the Court came to call at my home one evening. They insisted that we have an officiating ceremony with Court proclamations, burning candles, pledges of allegiance, official title naming ceremonies, definition of roles, and, of course, Confidentiality Agreements. We were crazy, middle-aged ladies and loving every minute of it!

So, who were we? Let's start with the perfect title: Lady Jester. I have never known anyone with such a quick wit and sharp mind; her caustic responses to events were so spontaneous, so well timed. If Lady Jester could not make you laugh, you were hopeless.

Then there's Duchess, my lifelong friend, always a vigilant supporter of everyone, twinkling eyes, selfless, clever, devilish with the South Carolina accent, insightful, and game for anything.

And now, Principessa, a most extraordinary, larger-than-life-personality. Principessa is the glue of the Court, the designer of the brand, the creative genius among us and the absolutely greatest comedic writer in the world.

And then there's me, tq, the instigator of adventures and the inventive party planner. Together, we were a powerhouse in the kingdom of unending imagination.

What ensued was a series of madcap adventures and witty and boisterous dinner celebrations. We were nearly thrown out of several restaurants due to gales of uncontrolled laughter. Together, we were rowdy and unrestrained. WE WERE BOLD, BRASH AND BEAUTIFUL, wrapped in a relationship of trust.

And the ties that bind were all about the gifts – funny, inexpensive gifts, crazy rhinestone pins, bracelets, and, of course, tiaras. According to the rules of the court, (which were signed documents), we were required to wear our tiaras at all official court meetings (held both publicly or privately), and yes, we did! While we enjoyed several more weekends in New York, it's hard to remember when we had the most fun – on the trips there and back or the dinners. Or was it the hilarious tricks we played on each other? We were unabashedly celebrating life itself in a carefree, dedicated time, sharing stories, friendships and unforgettable moments, including an exchange of a secret prize that would somehow show up at every event (or sometimes in-between!).

The most useful companion on our adventures was the camera, but the best results were the photos shared. Occasionally photos somewhat mysteriously appeared singularly or in albums with captions reflecting the essence of this zany royal Court. The photos captured the moment; the inventive captions replayed the hilarity; this is the stuff that memories are made of. Some of our most famous photos were snapped at an ordinary parking lot outside of a rest stop on the New Jersey turnpike. We each took our turn standing in the center of the car, rooftop open, hands waving to the fictitious crowds with crowns on. In my case, wig and crown! This classic framed memento hangs in my office today with the caption, "If the tiara fits!"

There are many stories that I cannot tell about the reunions of the Court (or it would be a violation of the Confidentiality Agreement!), but the Court has granted me permission to share this one specific moment.

As the formal party planner of the Court, I decided to hold a royal dinner party for no reason at all at my home, (in our terms: "one of the Palaces"), in my sleepy suburban community. And our husbands, now embraced as Dukes and Princes of various Principalities, were invited. There we were, eight of us dressed to the nines in gowns and tuxedos and feathers, and, naturally, everyone was required to wear a crown. (Mine was, of course, pinned to my wig!)

We had a wonderful dinner and an exchange of gifts (now the men were participating too!) and laughter abound. Each gift had an official presentation and frankly, one was funnier than the other; this was all about creativity, cleverness and humor.

And then...the doorbell rang. I got up from the table and answered the door only to discover a police officer (and a well-built and handsome one to boot) who just walked right in. What a scene we must have been! Eight crown-bearing adults completely decked out, just finishing the gift-giving ceremony in clear view of the front door. As the officer stepped in, it only took me seconds, then I knew! The Court had gone to the edge and hired a male stripper! I promptly grabbed the shirtsleeve of the "policeman" and walked him directly to the dining table and the seated guests. I chidingly proclaimed aloud to the officer as I stood at his side, "Okay. I know this caper. I know who you are!"

Everyone cracked up, laughing to tears, some with heads in hands, some with heads on the table. They were uncontrollable; the bad behavior of the Court had been discovered in the nip of time by tq! I saved the day! HA! The Court was beyond hysterics because the joke was on me! This man was a real police officer! Apparently our security system had somehow sent out a silent alarm. Oh dear. The officer had to think I was crazy. I don't think I will ever live this incident down in my lifetime!

So why am I writing this chapter? I hope my subtle message is clear. Most of us know someone that has been diagnosed with something serious, and as a friend, you wonder hopelessly what to do. You feel powerless to help.

Well, you are not!

My friends took me on an adventure that helped to take my mind and body away from the unrelenting aspects of the cancer journey – the meds, the chemo, the surgeons, and the fear. Yes, my friends supported me in a unique way…they used humor as the weapon in the cancer battle. I would even receive humorous, loving gifts and cards at the clinic before a chemo infusion. And, I cannot talk about what showed up in hospital rooms!

As you are reading this, whoever you are, wherever you are, know that you can help those close to you at a time when they need you the most. Celebrate the treasure of being alive, laugh at life, find joy and humor, and above all, capture the moments together. Any diversion, however small, will be deeply appreciated. Luckily, the universe provides us all with an infinite variety of ideas.

These stories are true; they took place over a decade ago. I am convinced that medical intervention healed my body, but my friends healed my soul.

SUZANNE GABLI

Suzanne Gabli is a visionary whose strengths are in relationships, leadership, and collaboration. Suzanne writes about vision, overcoming adversity, her own personal journey of reflection, early childhood education and that anything is possible.

Suzanne is the Owner and Executive Director of Building Blocks Preschool, An Early Childhood Community and nature based school in Highland, MI. Suzanne has a published article about the connection between the child and the Reggio Emilia Approach to learning.

Suzanne also works in the print and marketing field since 1991. As a marketing strategist, she assists organizations in creating useful, purposeful marketing projects for her clients.

✉ **suzannegabli@gmail.com**

⌂ **www.BuildingBlocksSchool.com**

⌂ **www.DBSPrintMarketing.com**

f **www.facebook.com/suzanne.gabli**

⌂ **www.twitter.com/suzannegabli1**

in **www.linkedin.com/in/suzannegabli**

CHAPTER 13

ANYTHING IS POSSIBLE

By Suzanne Gabli

"You can conquer almost any fear if you will only make up your mind to do so. For remember, fear doesn't exist anywhere except in the mind."

– Dale Carnegie

Are you afraid of possibilities? Of failure? Think about it. What are you afraid of?

Everyone is afraid of something. It could be something that most would consider insignificant, such as heights, spiders or change. Or it could be a major life challenge: rejection, illness, starting a new business, changing jobs, running for office, success, death or – what people are said to fear worse than death – public speaking!

What would it mean to you if you could get over those fears, or at least take a step back and be less afraid to examine them? Are you brave and bold enough to face them and live your heart's desire? I know that whenever I conquer one of my fears, I experience a feeling of freedom that anything is possible and nothing is going to hold me back.

My father was a self-employed real estate entrepreneur, while mom went to school to finish her biology and chemistry degree. They wanted a better and more stable life for their family. One had an entrepreneur's risk taking spirit, and the other wanted the consistency of a paycheck and benefits.

Although they had strong faith and deep love for their family, it was a constant struggle for them to make ends meet, and issues ensued with addiction, stress and a failed marriage. As a result, life for me was inconsistent and instilled a deep fear that I would let my loved ones down. I became the pleaser, and entered adolescence and then adulthood highly afraid of failure.

As an adult, I can look back without regret because those adverse childhood experiences created within me a strong drive for success. I have learned how to think big and have been determined to break free from real and perceived limitations, such as those that held my parents back. I made sure my children were not raised in an atmosphere of uncertainty, instability and low self-worth. Instead, I have taught them to feel powerful, be resourceful, and to set goals for what they want with confidence that they will succeed. I want them to see the world as Anything is Possible.

I was fortunate to have had wonderful mentors in my youth, people who I could count on to help me sort my thoughts and begin to realize my dreams. One of them shared with me that there are three kinds of people: "I" people, "Us" people and "We" people. He said, "Suzanne, you are a 'We' person." At the time it perplexed me, but I never forgot his words. Over time, I found that he was right. I am a "We" person. I absolutely believe in the "Power of We" and that together "we" can accomplish so much more than "I".

All of my life I've had this gut feeling that I could make a difference in the lives of others in my community. It's been said, "Life is a journey, not a destination." I want to live a life full of adventure, surrounded by captivating people and the joy of children, loving and being loved. That's why I became an advocate for child and adult literacy and for children's rights. I visualized children developing in much-deserved, richly natural surroundings, experiencing wonder and joy in their learning setting. In my vision, all children are smart and are allowed the time to explore their strengths in a safe, warm and positive environment. I was confident and determined that this vision would come true. I would provide a strong foundation of healthy experiences for children to be centered on their strengths and their own self-expressions of who they are and who they want to be.

In 2004, my husband proposed a life-changing event – buying the early childhood learning center my children attended. I thought he was crazy! He was self-employed, I was working full time, and we had two small children. However, when we found we were expecting number three, I felt a nudge of divine encouragement to move forward, to realize my vision of offering a higher quality education, a sense of community where children would be treated with respect, and a place to create memories of wonder, joy and nature.

We purchased an old farmhouse and developed our school, which backs up to 5,000 acres of natural state land and currently serves 45 children. We researched the schools of Reggio Emilia, Italy, one of the most innovative, high-quality city-run infant-toddler and pre-primary systems in the world. Drawing from the ideas of many great thinkers, the belief is that a child has the right to be an active constructor of knowledge and a social being. Instituting this system in our school, classrooms are aesthetic, children's work is sophisticated, and parent involvement is high – a truly holistic approach to learning.

The start of a big vision came with a big investment, including home equity, property sales, life savings, and our own monthly income. We were overcommitted, and the 2008-12 economic downturn took a toll. We needed to seek council in three key areas - finance, marriage, and faith. We survived the perils the hard times brought thanks to our mutual love and support, a dynamic teaching staff, family, friends, mentors, retirement savings and the grace of God.

During those dark times, I still believed in the vision, and therefore knew I would have to make some life changing decisions that would test just how bold and committed I was to it. These are the times that springboard your purpose and empower you in every area of life. My journey led from my heart to my head and back to my heart again. In those times when I was heart-centered, I rediscovered the universe of possibility and my strengths as an "all in" kind of person.

Our school's success is now being recognized more in our community. It has taken time, vision, leadership, and the synergy of an amazing teaching staff that is open and willing to be on a journey of exploration and life long learning, collaboration, a deep respect for children, the creation every day of wonder and joy, and, of course, the belief that Anything is Possible.

Lessons learned are too many to name, but they all started with releasing fear, guilt and the little girl who needed to please everyone else. I had to go deep to find the core of who I am and to believe that I am enough; that when I am clear about my desires, dreams, passions and the core of "why I am here," I have what it takes to walk my path and succeed. This was a process and it took time and the help of an amazing life coach who helped me with clarity, and who dug deep to see what was inside all along.

Your passion is ignited by your purpose in life, and your mission and vision enable you to apply that spark to change your world. You have the answers inside your heart. In business and in life, surround yourself with those who have strong core values that resonate with your vision. Believe in the power of "We" and that together Anything is Possible.

"At first people refuse to believe that a strange new thing can be done, then they begin to hope it can be done, then they see it can be done – then it is done and all the world wonders why it was not done centuries ago."

– The Secret Garden

TRISHA HARNER

Trisha Harner is the founder of It's Your Life, Create It! Through workshops and one-on-one coaching, she helps people tap into their authentic creative selves – creating empowering self-awareness and positive changes in careers, health, and relationships. Organizations, entrepreneurs, families, and individuals benefit from her proven methods for opening up creative centers and integrating the right and left brain. Her clients are guided to find their true desired goals and work toward these visions.

She's studied under Lucia Capacchione, PhD, ATR, REAT, originator of Creative Journal Expressive Arts (CJEA) and Visioning®. A Certified CJEA Instructor, and trained Visioning® Coach, Harner lives in Midland, Michigan, with her husband and two teenage daughters.

To discover what your heart desires and begin creating it with the unique visioning methods I share, you can sign up to receive a free six step vision board audio guide at www.trishaharner.com.

🏠 www.trishaharner.com

f www.facebook.com/Trisha.Harner.1

🐦 www.twitter.com/trishaharner

ⓟ www.pinterest.com/trishaharner/boards

📷 www.instagram.com/trisha_harner

www.linkedin.com/pub/trisha-harner/23/616/57b/

www.youtube.com/channel/UCL71ScdHbOo71pTPnGZK7LQ/feed

CHAPTER 14

$\mathscr{S}$TEP OUT OF THE BOX, CREATE YOUR HEART'S DESIRE

By Trisha Harner

Have you ever wondered, "Is this it?"

I have, and boy, I was bothered big time when life hit me with this question. Every point that had led me to a certain time in my life was really good. I had two beautiful daughters, a good job, a loving hardworking husband, a cozy home, friends and family, but there was a nagging feeling that there was *more* – like I had time to even consider what *more* meant. My plate was full, and I had loads of laundry to fold on top of it.

Yet one day, a special woman lying in a bed in a nursing home opened her deep brown eyes, stared up into mine and she asked, "Trisha, how did I get here?"

I stared back at her with words stuck in my throat, as visions swirled around in my head of how she indeed got to be "here."

My husband, her only child, while visiting one day, learned that she no longer was going to her scheduled doctor appointments.

Even under her concerned doctor's care, loving supportive husband, family and friends, this stubborn mother-in-law of mine had stopped eating and taking her anti-depressants months ago. The tests had been run, and they couldn't find one single cause for her symptoms. All the doctor could do was treat her for depression and pain with pills.

On a sunny July day just one month before her 63rd birthday, we won the battle of delivering her unharmed to the hospital, but there was no victory party. Her condition was beyond our care, and we were left with no other choice but to seek professional help against her will.

It was the last time she'd ever see the house as we drove down the very road she had driven back and forth a thousand times taking my husband to school, his baseball games, to her work, the grocery store, and to visit friends and family.

Her hospital stay extended to the nursing home and within three weeks she died in that very bed that she had asked me her question. This is the moment something in me switched over from how I had known life and sparked a desire of how I wanted to experience *more*. At the time I didn't know what it meant, but I felt a knowing awaken within me that things were going to change.

I had started to feel trapped in a job that served me well, but was one I didn't care for anymore, and my denial of this fact started to manifest as neck pain so unbearable I was forced to take time off of work to heal; only it was eventually diagnosed as chronic pain; aka, suck it up, you'll have it forever so get back to work!

Anxiety set in and I truly thought I was going to die from panic attacks I was experiencing daily. I would burden my neighboring co-workers, informing them what my symptoms were in case I keeled over and they had to call 911.

Worst of all, my daughters were witnessing my negative complaints, low energy, and lack of joy in my work. Having witnessed their grandmother's light within slowly fade as her heart got drowned out through all the regrets, anger, and disappointments in life, her dying was my wake up call.

It was from there that I leapt out of my 23 year career, stumbling along my new path open to discovery; I poured my soul into my search for *more*.

I unburied my writing passion by joining a writer's group and gained support from other women searching for their *more* in self-help book

100

discussions where I learned there are no accidents or coincidences, only one synchronicity after another showing us the way to experience life the way we are meant to.

Gratefully, I was led to learn and train in work as a certified Creative Journal Expressive Art Instructor and Vision Coach that I'm thrilled to be sharing with women ready to step out of the box as they begin to answer the question, "Is this it?'

The conscious awareness methods I share are a subtle whole brain integration that re-pattern the nervous system and other aspects of the physical body. By becoming emotionally aware and shifting internal energy that unblocks us, we are able to use visioning to tap into what we know in our own heart, and are empowered to create desired experiences.

As a Vision Coach I often hear this question, "What if my husband doesn't like what my heart desires?"

When we boldly own what it is we desire to create, it makes for beautiful new beginnings, even when taking chances is uncomfortable. I know from experience that a marriage can upheave when we start to explore outside the box, visioning what our heart truly desires can rock relationships to the core.

Personally, I wasn't willing to sacrifice myself to keep him comfortable. Determined to experience what my heart was calling, I sought out supportive women. Those who see our greatness are important because change is never easy for anyone, especially when we start to truly nurture, protect and honor our heart.

Visioning is magical, but it doesn't happen overnight. Poof... all better! Refreshed marriage, new career, healthy body! Nope, it takes work; but it so worth it!

When I stepped out of the box, even during the chaos and dark times of uncertainty, I felt totally alive! When we are aligned with our heart, we have incredible strength within us to create our own experiences that the heart is whispering to us every day to live out. We just have to honor and trust that everyone, even doubting husbands, will benefit when we listen.

It still takes huge doses of self-love to continue on the course of what it is I desire to experience, as well as discipline, patience and persistence.

What I have learned and what I teach is to practice three main forms of taking time for oneself in order to build a foundation to stay grounded, clear and focused no matter what commotion is going on around you.

1. Practice of Gratitude – Every day write down 2 to 3 things that you're grateful for. I don't care how mundane it may seem, toothpaste on the toothbrush, a cool breeze, anything; there must be 2 to 3 things you can feel good about each day!

2. Practice of "do nothing" – Take 2- 5 minutes a day to sit and do nothing! Just letting thoughts float in, but not getting up to fold the laundry. Sit. Feel the difference as energy shifts. There may be a new perspective of what really needs to be done next in the day or it creates a fresh boost of energy to complete tasks.

3. Practice of a "selfie date" – Just you and your creative self hanging out doing whatever you please. Maybe a walk, taking in a movie, sticker shopping, making banana bread, just listen and honor whatever it may be and have some fun doing it all by yourself.

I know how it goes, have an ache or low energy…push it down, push through; there is no time for that right now. We're all so busy, aren't we? That darn laundry. When we do this, our inner child screams for attention; and if we choose to ignore the body's discomforts and unhealthy emotions, we are not showing strength, boldness or loyalty to our employer, co-workers, children, parents or even our husbands. There is no beauty in it at all.

My mother-in-law's negative, angry, ungrateful thoughts consumed her soul and she stopped feeling what the heart desired to experience. Although I now look at her death as a teaching moment that awakened me to start thriving in my own life, I can't help but wonder what life would have been like for her if she had listened to her heart.

I've experienced the healing of my own chronic health issues (yes, that pain in the neck is in check), recharged my marriage without sacrificing me, created my life's work, and now witness the same outcome for those who I touch with this methodology of visioning and Creative Journal Expressive Arts successfully in my business.

What we think is what we get, and I am determined to share with women that connecting the whole mind with the heart through visual affirmations, emotional awareness, and positive thoughts is a magical, powerful methodology. It can literally change the DNA and create a new future for those who follow in our footsteps. I don't want any woman, especially my daughters, to have to look anyone in the eye one day and ask, "How did I get here?"

So beware! Creative journals and vision collages fill with messages of feelings that unblock and inspire the desire to LIVE and THRIVE in a life created by you, and will cause these long lasting side effects: Feelings of joy, gratitude, happiness, fulfillment, energy, love, hope and inner peace.

Create your heart's desire!

The world needs women to know that bold is beautiful. It's your life, create it!

TERRY WILDEMANN, CEC, CPCC

An entrepreneur in the professional development industry for 30 years, business alchemist and intuitive leader, Terry Wildemann, gets to the root of her clients self-sabotaging issues with her seasoned and expert business and career building wisdom and coaching. Terry's work results in her clients quickly improving their clarity, self- esteem, personal and workplace performance and communications leading to business growth and profit due to their improved intuitive leadership skills. A certified executive and co-active coach, Licensed Heartmath® Provider for stress management, EFT/Tapping coach, certified law of attraction trainer, certified professional behavior analyst, and Reiki Master, Terry has presented and worked nationally and internationally with thousands of professionals and entrepreneurs in the military, for profit and non-profit companies, holistic and small businesses.

She is a co-author of two international bestselling books, "Success in High Heels" and "Hot Mama in High Heels," co-author of "Unlock the Power of You," and author of "1-800-Courtesy; Connecting With a Winning Telephone Image"

Connect with Terry!

Heart Centered Success

✉ **TerryWildemann@gmail.com**

🏠 **www.TerryWildemann.com**

📞 **(401) 849 5900**

Follow me at:

f **www.facebook.com/TerryWildemann**

f **www.facebook.com/HeartCenteredSuccess**

in **www.linkedin.com/in/terrywildemann**

y **www.twitter.com/terrywildemann**

CHAPTER 15

ℰVOLVING INTO AN UNSTOPPABLE INTUITIVE LEADER

By Terry Wildemann

Truly successful leaders tap into their intuition and access all of their skills to bring out the best in others. It's about belief and trust in oneself and the passion to make a difference in the lives of those we are meant to lead.

At a young age, I understood the importance of great leadership, the responsibility involved in influencing others, and the importance of putting people first. According to Wikipedia, leadership has been described as "a process of social influence in which one person can enlist the aid and support of others in the accomplishment of a common task." It truly takes skill to influence others to do the right thing at the right time to create positive results in the workplace and life.

Leaders come in all shapes and sizes, and most of my workplace managers taught me well what not to do in a leadership role. However, in my personal and entrepreneurial life, and in my role as a military spouse, there are quite a few leaders who influenced me beyond what I thought possible.

These intuitive leaders allowed me to grow with them. We learned from one another in amazing ways that allowed each of us to shine! They taught me to lead those around me with passion, purpose and drive. I learned to make a difference by listening to my intuitive heart and doing what I believed was right. When the folks I led smiled, performed well, felt safe, and were happy; I knew I had made a difference in their lives – and they had made a difference in mine.

Who are these people who influenced me so much?

First, my wonderful husband, who always amazes me. When I think of great leadership, this is the person who immediately comes to mind. We are likeminded in values and leadership, and understand that people accomplish tasks. Blending a strategic mind with an empathic heart creates management success – and he has the gift. He is whom I go to for guidance when I'm stuck, and in need of an objective person to guide me.

Walt's ability to look at issues with a 360-degree objectivity is why he's a leader's leader. A 25-year military veteran, his practical, intuitive, honest and no-nonsense approach makes it clear that he understands that emotions drive people. He respects those who work with him and for him, and that trait is critical to creating positive workplace results. Every day, he teaches me something, whether it's with business advice or in handling a family matter. He makes me laugh and shows me clearly the outcomes of the path I'm taking, and darn it – he tends to be right! Thanks, Love of My Life!

The second influential leader was my military guide and first Commanding Officer's spouse. When it came to leadership, she taught me what being a supportive military spouse was about. This amazing woman took me under her wing, and we connected in a deep way. We thought alike, supported each other, and supported other spouses where we could. She held me accountable in a loving way, and taught me all I needed to know when it was my turn to be the Captain's spouse. Believe me, there was a lot to learn. Nancy taught me the art of diplomacy, team building, listening, taking inspired action and following my gut instincts. She taught me how to create something from nothing, and how to support without getting overly involved so others stayed independent. She taught me how to lead from my heart.

Thirdly, my business mentor, who to this day teaches me so much! His advice always focuses on people and helping them be the best they can be. We constantly talk about intuition, doing the right thing, and creating outcomes that change lives. Jim is the ultimate customer

COMPILED BY **KIM BOUDREAU SMITH**

service professional, and it's because of him that several of my business models exist today.

And, finally, my Dad. Cuban daughters traditionally stay at home until married. Well, this Cubanita was having no part of that act! My career goal was to go into law enforcement, and much to my parents chagrin, it happened. There was one influential event that stands out to me as an intuitive leader. As I was about to go into an interview for a police department, a meltdown came from nowhere. Like many who suddenly realize their dream is becoming a reality, the fear was overwhelming and walking away was about to happen! This was the first time something I had worked for so hard was coming true. I called my dad in hysterics, and he gently brought me down from the self-sabotage, encouraging me to follow my heart and to go do what I worked for. I got the job and a lesson to remember.

There's one phrase my dad always says that is imprinted firmly in my memory, "You get a lot more with honey than with vinegar." He repeated it again and again, and it keeps me grounded and reminds me to treat people with respect.

The lesson of treating people with honey apparently escaped my first manager who was a master of leading with vinegar. At the age of 16, I was a women's shoes sales associate. Customer service is in my DNA, and intuitively it made sense that if every customer was served to the best of my ability, they would come back. Imagine my surprise when one day this manager, an unhappy guy who wanted everyone around him to be as miserable as he, fired me because I spent too much time with the customer! Really? Well, I walked next door to Woolworth's and applied for a job as a waitress. I was hired on the spot. Two weeks later, while washing down the counter at my new job, I looked up and saw my old manager walking towards me. The words that came out his mouth shocked and pleased me at the same time. He asked, "Would you come back to work for me?" "Why," I asked? He responded with, "The customers keep asking for you and want only you." Hmmm.

Going back to the shoe store intuitively didn't feel right, so that was a "no-brainer" of a decision. Understanding how a negative manager could create unnecessary chaos and pain by firing me for doing my job was mind-blowing and felt awful. The ability to boldly take charge and manifest a new job immediately was liberating. Learning and understanding that when a manager starts the chain of delivering great service by treating his employees well, they, in turn, serve the customer well. The result was something I already intuitively knew: that happy employees and repeat customers increase profits. What an absolutely enlightening and validating leadership and customer service experience for a 16 year old!

After I graduated from college with a Criminal Justice degree, it was a challenge to find a job in my field. My friend Kali and I applied for server positions at a new restaurant that was opening, and we were hired. Within 3 months, Kali became the dining room manager, and I was the assistant dining room manager and continued on as a server.

The promotion caused the true Kali to emerge. She transformed overnight into a key swinging, "yes, I'm in charge," control freak diva.

This company had very high standards and in the evenings, the glassware and silverware were highly polished and the table set for the next day. The dining room manager on duty was to inspect each server's station top to bottom before the server could leave for the night. This is where Kali sealed her reputation of being one of the most disliked people on the planet. This once-upon-a-time-server loved pointing out what was "imperfect." She then perched herself on a chair and watched until it was time to review the station again. Often we were there until 1 am because of this woman.

On my watch as the dining room manager, I cleared tables when busy, helped the team serve meals to our guests, and ensured my fellow servers and our guests got great service. At the end of the night I would point out what needed extra attention at each station and helped whenever possible so we left at a decent hour. For me, that leadership role was purely about support instead of control.

One day I noticed that very few servers scheduled themselves when Kali was on duty. Yet, on my two days as manager it was full. I commented on that and one of the lead servers took me aside and explained that because I treated my co-workers with respect, everyone wanted to work with me. The energy in the restaurant was different when I was the leader. WOW!

I'm grateful to Kali because she allowed me to witness and experience at a young age how the "command and control" style of leadership demeans people and creates a negative workplace culture.

My intuitive leadership style supports and respects people, thus allowing them to thrive. In that job I learned that leading and managing meant supporting where possible, and that when everyone works together, work gets done quickly, efficiently and to high standards.

Blending the lessons from these early experiences and those taught by my teachers has allowed me to create a powerful alchemy of success. By merging high performing values of trust, honor and respect with logic, tactics, positive communications, energy and spirituality, I am the bold and unstoppable intuitive leader of today that loves spreading the message of service.

BOLD IS BEAUTIFUL

BARBARA J. EISELE MC, NCC, PCC

Barbara is the founder and Chief Inspiration Officer of Life Transformations, Now! She is a transformational coach, inspirational speaker and international bestselling author. Through her own life experiences she has traveled the sacred transformational journey to discover the many layers of her Authentic Brilliance. Having evolved through three professional careers, she now lives her purpose by guiding other women in the process of discovering and living from the "sweet spot" of their Authentic Self.

🏠 www.lifetransformationsnow.com

✉ barb@lifetransformationsnow.com

f www.facebook.com/LifeTransformationsNow

🐦 www.twitter.com/barbeisele

📌 www.pinterest.com/barbaraeisele

▶ www.youtube.com/BarbaraEisele

📞 (520) 977 0562

CHAPTER 16

*B*E BOLD: LET YOUR LIGHT SHINE

By Barbara Eisele

"You aren't REALLY going to say that are you? Are you crazy! Don't do it; it's not going to help anyone anyway," My inner critic was barking at me. It was relentless. The knot in my stomach twisted tighter and tighter. My throat was rapidly closing. My pounding heart felt like there was a hammer in my chest. It had to be visible to the women waiting to hear me speak. The room was a blur as I listened to the MC read my introduction. I didn't know if my legs would hold me as I rose from my chair and started to walk forward.

I had agreed to talk about "The Power of Your 'Big Why'." When I made the commitment, I thought I knew what I was going to say. I'd given the talk before and it had been well received. I had no idea that by the date of the talk I would find myself sharing some of my biggest obstacles and most debilitating beliefs. Dealing with them had reignited my passion for my Big Why and made my previous talk seem flat and shallow. My intuition kept telling me I needed to share this deeper story for my own healing and to give others strength and hope for their life altering journey. This was the first time I was going to share the depth of my story with anyone beyond my inner most circle of friends. I was terrified.

Four months previously our dream home had gone to foreclosure. I had maintained a rational "I'm fine" attitude on the outside, but my interior world had been far different. I was devastated and despondent. If there was a loving Universe that was "for" me I saw no evidence of it. In desperation, I finally reached out to my husband and three dear girlfriends for support. When I did, I found love, compassion and some "kick butt" wisdom. It gave me strength to be intentional and consistent in my journey to answer the questions, "Who am I?" "What's the meaning of my life?" and "Why am I here?" I knew this was what I had to share.

In the days before the talk, I questioned my sanity a hundred times a day. How could I bare my soul and stand emotionally naked in front of 30 women? As I stood in my office rehearsing my talk, I pictured myself in front of the room. I was so nervous my mouth was completely dry; it made it difficult to speak the truth of my anguish and pain. The voice in my head kept saying, "This is not a good idea. If you just be quiet, no one ever has to know." The inner war raged on between my head and my heart. From my soul I knew this was what I needed to do, but I didn't have a clue how I was going get through it.

With sweaty palms and a halting voice I started the talk honestly and vulnerably. I shared that my usual way of speaking was to make sure that I "looked good" in front of the audience. I went on to say that today I was going to do it differently. I was going to expose the warts of my journey to reigniting my passion for my "Big Why." At that moment I took a deep breath and I felt like the audience did too. I could feel the openness in the room and all eyes were intently on me. I was still scared, but I was being completely authentic and inviting them to do the same.

I could never have imagined the outpouring of love I received after the talk. People hugged and thanked me for being so vulnerable. Words like courageous, resilient, and inspirational dominated the feedback I received. I was overwhelmed and humbled.

Exposing myself in this way proved to be a turning point in my journey and my life.

Over the next several months, unexpected opportunities began to show up. I saw more opportunities to be bold. One of them came in a conversation with a friend. She told me about an anthology that was being published by a woman in Spain. I found myself making an inquiry about writing a chapter in that book. She initially wrote back that all the slots were filled. I didn't think a whole lot about it and went on with my life. Then one day, I received an email from her saying that a woman couldn't fulfill her commitment and would I like to take her place. I remember reading the email several times. "Oh my god, can this be true?" While my brain was still trying to figure out if it was real, I said yes!

I knew the story I would tell. It would be what I didn't say in my talk some months before. The Universe was giving me a chance to choose to be bolder, tell the whole story and reach a much larger audience through the book. This time I had a little more confidence, but being more vulnerable was still nerve racking. At the same time, I had greater passion for others to find hope in the dark. I want all women to overcome whatever is stopping them from bringing forth their Authentic Brilliance and letting it shine for themselves and others.

I developed a wonderful collaborative relationship with the other authors in the book. We had a strategy for publicizing the book on the day of the launch. Through social media, we communicated with each on a moment-to-moment basis. At times I was speechless because it was so beyond anything I had ever done. Never had I been so clear I wasn't alone, that we were in this together. Emotionally I vacillated between tears of joy and giddy disbelief that we were really doing this. I still relish the experience of immense pride and elation as we climbed to number one on Amazon in several categories, "Yes, we did it!" I became an international bestselling author!

I found my Spirit renewed. The internal experience is almost impossible to describe. I felt vibrant, expansive and free, like I could fly. I was very proud of myself. Being bold had broken the chains that bound me. I hadn't felt this alive and powerful in years.

This was an opportunity for life to never be the same again, but it was up to me. I knew that the hype, accolades and all the external excitement of the book would subside quickly. So on the day after the book was launched I sat in the early morning light with my journal and pen asking myself, "Who am I inside as a result of this accomplishment? How did I get here just a year after feeling life was hopeless? What's next?"

116

Along with gratitude, the word that kept coming to me was courageous. The Latin root of the word "courage" is *cor* and means "the heart." At one time it meant, "to speak all that is in one's heart." My more contemporary definition of courage is "action in the face of fear." On reflection of the old and new definitions, I realize my intuition was pushing me to speak from my heart while feeling terrified. Fear will always be a part of life, but I don't have to let it stop me. Being bold calls us to know what's in our heart, face our fear and step into action. It's a way of being that is generated from the inside and manifested in action on the outside. When I listened to my intuition and shared more vulnerably without succumbing to the voices of doubt and fear, I was bold.

Writing the chapter for my first anthology was only one of several transformational opportunities that showed up as a result of my boldness. Some of them seemed small. For example, giving up when something like posting a video confounds me because of my limited knowledge of technology. Saying "I can do this" and asking for help was bold. When it was finally posted, I give myself a pat on the back, "Yes, I did it."

This new bold way of being is integrated into my daily life. Sometimes it surprises me. I am taking on bigger projects and what I once believed were pipe dreams I now visualize as possible. I've learned that I don't have to know how it is going to come about, I just have to see the end result, feel positive expectancy that it will come and take the first step.

I know that before long I will be called to the edge of my new boldness and will have to go through the discomfort of stepping forward and being courageous. I don't know what it will be, but if I listen to my heart it will lead me to the next bold move that has my Authentic Brilliance, my Light, shine in the world.

ARIANA LISE NEWCOMER

Ariana Lise Newcomer is a Transformational Voice Coach and the developer of the Reclaim Your Authentic Voice™ programs and Bodywork for the Voice^{SM}. Ariana teaches coaches, conscious entrepreneurs and others to own and voice their value, speak confidently from their authentic selves, and communicate powerfully for dramatically successful public speaking.

She is a Harvard graduate, former professional opera singer, Massage Therapist, a Certified Provider of The Listening Program®, mom of two, and has taught voice since 1995. A voice injury ended her singing career, and her journey back to a healthy voice, along with her rich performing, teaching and therapeutic background, inspired her unique and powerful approach to transformational voice coaching.

She believes passionately in the power of the human voice and our ability to grow, change and develop through reclaiming our authentic voices. Change your voice, change your life, change the world!

🔗 www.linkedin.com/in/ariananewcomer

🏠 www.reclaimyourauthenticvoice.com

f www.facebook.com/ReclaimYourAuthenticVoice

CHAPTER 17

RECLAIM YOUR AUTHENTIC VOICE

By Ariana Lise Newcomer

They say that for singers, losing your voice is like losing a limb. It certainly felt like it at the time.

I became a classical singer in my mid-thirties. That's late to start a singing career, but I managed it. I juggled two small children, voice lessons, doing some bodywork, teaching singing, and performing. I sang principal roles in regional opera and as a soloist with area symphonies and ensembles.

I loved it. I was certain it was THE THING that Spirit meant for me to do in the world. Using my voice with such expression and control in the service of beautiful music was my greatest joy. It was my fullest expression of my true self. It was my most direct connection with the divine.

One day my choir director called me into her office after rehearsal. She told me other singers were saying I was having pitch problems. This was news to me! I had never had pitch problems before. It was devastating and humiliating. It turned out I couldn't hear when I wasn't on pitch in a certain part of my range. I had to leave the group, and my singing career was over.

A couple of years later, so was my marriage.

I have always been one to follow my heart, trust my inner promptings, and follow my own path. (I can't say I always did the right thing, but that's another story.)

As a teenager, I found a way to spend my junior year of high school in Ireland. I went to college at Harvard. I was a professional modern dancer for 9 years in New York City. After my first marriage broke up, I moved with a boyfriend across the country, away from my whole family, to a place where I knew almost no one, and created a whole new life. Two years later, I got out of that emotionally abusive relationship (part of the other story), met and married my second husband. We have two wonderful boys who are the center of my heart.

Life was going a certain way – I was married, raising kids, singing, teaching, moving into a future that looked secure. When I lost my voice AND my marriage of 15 years, my whole world shifted. I felt like a failure. I didn't know what to do and I was terrified. Where was the person who had done those intrepid things in my past? Who was I now?

Being in a dysfunctional marriage (and the previous emotionally-abusive relationship) had made me stop trusting my own truth and inner knowing. I stopped believing in my own worth. I bought into the devaluing of my abilities, my importance, and my sensitivities. I bought into the devaluing of my work as a mother caring for our children and our home, and volunteering at their schools.

I would lie in bed sometimes crying, "I was meant to do something more in the world! How could I have gotten so far in my life and have so little to show for it?"

When I lost my singing voice, I felt I had lost a core part of myself. I now realize I had used performing to confirm my value as a person because I didn't feel valued in my marriage. Spirit had to take my performing away from me to get my attention. The loss of my singing voice was an external sign of the loss of my inner voice. It was a big neon sign from the universe, saying, "Your life is out of integrity! You have to change!"

The person I had been was an identity I had constructed. It was a false one. I had forgotten, buried and silenced important parts of myself to try to keep the marriage going, and to try to keep being the mom I wanted to be.

My journey to reclaim my voice and my value has been a long one, and the process of regaining my singing voice has dovetailed with reclaiming my authentic voice in the world. In fact, I feel like I am fully claiming my authentic voice for the first time.

Getting my voice back required a lot of different steps. In my marriage, I often metaphorically "swallowed" things I really needed to say. I'm not saying I didn't argue or fight – I did. But I didn't find a way to actually *communicate* the fundamentally important things.

Not only that, I didn't acknowledge that my marriage was undermining and damaging me. But my body did. It gave me acid reflux. Getting a divorce and being treated with homeopathy healed that.

Next, I had to re-train my self-listening (my ability to hear my own voice accurately) so I could hear when I wasn't on pitch. I did this through specialized therapeutic music programs and ear/voice training based on the work of Dr. Alfred Tomatis.

I also took the Estill Voice Training, which gave me an understanding of the anatomy and physiology of the voice, and how to use and teach different styles of singing and speaking while keeping the voice healthy.

The next step was releasing habits of tension in my tongue, jaw, neck and diaphragm that kept my voice from working freely. I was lucky to find a teacher who combines hands-on work with vocal technique and speech therapy exercises.

All along, I did the deeper work of rebuilding my confidence, and reclaiming my worth and value. I reconnected to my spiritual self and divine guidance. I did energy work to clear and heal old patterns, especially in my third and fifth chakras. The third (solar plexus) is about personal power, and the fifth (throat), of course, is all about voice.

Spiritual work teaches us to look for the lessons in the hard things that happen. Looking back, I see that what looked like devastation became a huge learning experience that moved me out of an inauthentic life into a rich, authentic, evolutionary one.

Everything I did in my journey to my authentic self and my authentic voice, combined with my rich performing, teaching and therapeutic background, has come together in my own work and business, Reclaim Your Authentic Voice™. I am so honored to do this work.

I teach conscious women entrepreneurs and authors to own and voice their value, release blocks to full self-expression, align their inner voice with their outer voice, and speak with power and confidence from their authentic selves.

Being an entrepreneur with integrity demands continual growth and ongoing transformation. It has called me into a larger work than I ever imagined when I was lying in bed crying that I was meant to do something bigger.

I am on a mission to change the world. Really.

I'm talking about worldwide cultural transformation: To create societies where people work in partnership with (rather than domination over) each other and our natural environment. Where men and women are truly equals, and our culture values the activities of caring that are currently given no value in our economic models and policies – caring for our children, caring for each other, and caring for our planet.

These larger issues were at play in my story. The failure of my marriage wasn't just our fault - my husband's and mine. We had our issues and we weren't able to solve them. But part of why we couldn't solve them is we didn't recognize the underlying cultural conversation that drove our biggest conflicts.

It's a conversation that says, "women are like this" and "men are like that." It says that women are less important than men; that the work of caring for children is not valuable work; that caring for each other and our planet has no value; that financial wealth is the only real wealth.

Author and sociologist, Riane Eisler, has been an extremely important influence in my journey. My name, Ariana, came to me in 1989 after reading her book, "The Chalice and The Blade." The book shifted my perspective on what's possible for humanity. It shows there were peaceful, partnership cultures with women leaders in our past, and that war and domination are not inherently part of human nature.

Ariana is an ancient name for the Great Mother goddess. I called my name to me over 20 years ago. Mother Earth is now calling me to live that name. She is at a tipping point. If we continue as we have been, we will not survive. It is time and past time for us to create a world that works for everyone.

Women's voices are needed. Conscious men's voices raised in partnership are needed. YOUR voice is needed.

I call you to reclaim your authentic voice. Speak confidently and powerfully with it. Be bold. Change the cultural conversation. Demand that your relationships (personal and business) value partnership and the activities of caring.

Become a leader. Help create our cultural transformation into true partnership with ourselves, each other and with our planet.

We have so much work to do. Join us.

MARY JO KURTZ

Mary Jo Kurtz is a Certified Life Empowerment Coach, Holistic Health Counselor, member of the American Association of Drugless Practitioners and spiritual energy worker. Mary Jo has been called a visionary and called to lead from her earliest of years. She inspires others to use their voices to collectively bring peace and well being into the world. She is the founder of Wellnecessity, a company dedicated to empowering others to take charge of their health and their lives with alternative and preventative therapies.

Mary Jo embraces her ultimate mother energy as an adoring wife and mother of four. She blends her no-nonsense style with her love of laughter to approach life as a daring adventure. She lives her life as if "there are no mistakes only lessons" and inspires others to embrace their unique gifts, illuminate their purpose and live their life with passion.

✉ mjskurtz@wellnecessity.com

f www.facebook.com/maryjoskurtz

f www.facebook.com/pages/Wellnecessity/183844094972093

𝕏 www.twitter.com/wellnecessity

in www.linkedin.com/pub/mary-jo-kurtz/0/339/697

𝒫 www.pinterest.com/wellnecessity

📷 www.instagram.com/wellnecessity

CHAPTER 18

THE POWER OF THE "F" WORD

By Mary Jo Kurtz

For most years of my adult life "Bold" would clearly have been a word that many would associate with me. It was a personality feature accompanied with tenacious, dedicated, and determined, all characteristics I learned early in my career climbing the ladder on Wall Street. It was what brought me success in a time when women found it difficult to advance. I was a young female, focused and driven, just trying to make a mark in a male dominated world. Unfortunately, as time would have it, those characteristics ultimately drove me to near death. In the early years, there was not much I wouldn't have taken on. One "F" word, FEAR, was not an option. My philosophy was to put your head down and plow forward. When times got hard, I just worked harder. It was a time when big risks meant big rewards, plain and simple. It was bold! However, now, more than 20 years later, "boldness" has evolved.

So, here's where the real "F" word comes in. I've finally learned its power. The word is FAITH, and the faith that I am referring to is faith in ourselves and why we're here on earth. Faith is what ensures that we live our lives in alignment with our purpose. I know the word faith is not a word that many equate with boldness. At times, I too, have struggled with the word thinking it was passive and weak. Having more faith wasn't something I felt would make me more bold or powerful. However, I've realized that's a misconception. Now I believe that when we act with faith we become even more powerful and bold.

The definition of the word faith is "a strong belief or trust in someone or something." It can mean a belief in the existence of God or a system of religious beliefs. In the bible it says that "Faith is the assurance of things hoped for, the conviction of things not seen." So I ask you, does having a belief in something that cannot be seen seem weak to you? I don't think so! On the contrary, having faith in something that we cannot see is quite bold indeed! It's far more powerful than sheer grit and determination alone. Action with faith can move mountains with far less effort.

One question I often receive from clients is, "How do you know you're in alignment with your purpose?" First, I believe one of the easiest ways to see this is by noticing what's happening in your life. Has life thrown you a curveball or hard times? Maybe your health is declining or has changed. These struggles may be warning signs, reminders to listen and pay attention. These are often messages to heed. When we do, life begins to unfold for us, sometimes effortlessly and often in a direction different from where we were headed.

Over the years this lesson has repeated itself, but two times in particular were pivotal in getting me where I am today. During my early years I plowed through life at a pace that was neither healthy nor my path. I was in a fast track career in accounting and finance. These were areas that I studied, excelled and even enjoyed. I was married, a young mom with two babies. I was juggling it all, but it took a toll on my health. That same bold personality and relentless work ethic eventually became a curse. My body shut down and that career came to a screeching halt.

It took me a few years of struggling with a debilitating illness to see the path that was being laid out before me. I trudged through traditional medical treatments until I was near death. One day I was introduced to alternative treatments and Traditional Chinese Medicine. Intrigued and desperate, I started researching and learning. I became my own guinea pig. I saw my health improve and I began to decipher the meaning of what was going on. It forced me to take responsibility for my health and pay attention to the choices I was making. Eventually, with faith, I saw the path being laid before me. I had always desired to help others and be of service. Now it was being presented to me.

I began studying alternative healing and my second career began. I learned valuable lessons in the connection between our health and all aspects of our lives. Most importantly, I finally understood how when I ignored my health I was ignoring something much deeper, my inner self and my purpose.

Having faith in things we cannot see can be a real challenge! Patience has never been a strong point for me. However, I've learned that all I needed would be presented to me in time. I must stress here, it was never on my timetable. I also learned that life doesn't present lessons just once. They're often repeated and, as life would have it, I was reminded of this lesson again.

Over the years I have used my training as both a life coach and holistic health counselor along with different healing modalities to help others who struggle with illness and life challenges. My vision also includes broadening the scope of such work by supporting other practitioners like me in order to make alternative therapies more available and accepted in the world. However, like most small business owners, at first I struggled with how to do this. My financial background told me that it was important that practitioners like me diversify their income in order to sustain themselves. As a result, I spent four years learning and incorporating ecommerce into my business model with the hope to support others who needed the same. As you might guess, I turned to old habits working 24-7 and burning myself out. However, this time I knew enough to look for support and so I researched seemingly successful business coaches with similar backgrounds to me. I listened to why increased marketing efforts were the answer to grow my business. They told me how to build my list, create a sales funnel, and promised huge income jumps. I listened to the steps I NEEDED to follow, what my website and business MUST have. I was listening so hard, but I didn't hear my own voice inside. I ignored the fact that nobody was asking what MY vision was. When I asked questions about my ideas, I was told it wouldn't work, and to just follow their plan. So, I spent months and thousands of dollars following their rules.

It wasn't until it was excruciatingly painful that I had my "Aha Moment." I had hired this coach to create a new ecommerce site that would supposedly incorporate my vision. She assured me her team was well versed in ecommerce, and they could have it done quickly. For me, time was money. I was sold. Unfortunately, after five long months of beating my head against the wall, it became too painful to ignore. My bank account was empty and I still had no site. While it wasn't easy to admit I'd been fooled and lost thousands of dollars, it was worse yet to admit that I'd given away my voice, my passion and my power.

So, you might ask, "You're a coach. Why would you have chosen to work with someone like that?" I asked myself the same question. The answer was quite simple. I'd lost faith in myself, why I had started my business to begin with, and how much I really knew. I believed her when she told me she knew better than me what was right for me and my business. I was looking for an easy solution. You can probably relate. Have you ever had someone tell you what to do but it just didn't feel right? You felt that voice inside saying not to do it. Maybe you did it anyway. Maybe you didn't, but as I can attest, this is when we need to be bold, have faith in ourselves, and take our own action.

This is faith in action, and for all of us this is different. We are all unique beings with unique gifts and purpose. That's what sets us apart. That's why cookie cutter approaches won't make us successful. In truth, that is what makes coaching support so valuable. Authentic coaches won't tell a client what they MUST do. Coaches believe that each of us already has the answers within. They're just there to help you find them. When it happens, it's like magic.

Now, so much has changed for me since the early days of behaving like a bold woman in a man's world. Like many bold women in our history I've learned to incorporate BOLD FAITH into BOLD ACTIONS. This has made life much more enjoyable, less tenuous and an awesome ride. I encourage you to do the same. This same faith is inside you. Let it out. Become the person you are destined to be.

KIM BOUDREAU

Kim Boudreau, born Kimberley Lanceleve on June 2, 1965, in Nova Scotia, Canada, has always known she would someday be an entrepreneur. Shortly after graduating from high school in 1984 with a diploma in business; she and a partner started their first of many business ventures. Eventually, Kim found her way into retail and managed a successful jewellery and gift shop for many years. It was then that her passion for business blossomed. However, it would take a car accident to jolt Kim back to reality and remind her of the desire to own and operate her very own jewellery business.

Starting Kreative Design in 2010 has been a dream come true for Kim. In the first year, Kreative Design collectively raised over $15,000 for local charity and was nominated for several Excellence in Business Awards through the local Chamber of Commerce, winning "Best Ladies Boutique" in 2011 and "Best Place to Shop" in 2012.

Kim recognized the growing trend toward social media and in the beginning grew the boutique primarily through social media. Elevating Kreative Design to a "MUST SEE" Boutique with a dedicated following of over 3400 Facebook fans has been Kim's passion. Demonstrating the importance of social media and peer interaction as well as creating a unique shopping experience for her clients is at the forefront of her business, thus setting Kreative Design apart from its competitors.

- kreativedesign@kdx.ca
- www.twitter.com/KreativelyKim
- www.facebook.com/kreativedesign.net
- www.facebook.com/kimboudreau4
- ca.linkedin.com/in/kimboudreau1
- www.kreativedesign.net
- www.pinterest.com/KreativeDesigns/boards
- Skype: kreativelykim
- +1 (902) 578 6782
- Boutique Number: 1-902-567-0648
- www.youtube.com/channel/UCWlPml7upziohVNHS29B-Zg

CHAPTER 19

BOLD STEPS TO A BEAUTIFUL LIFE

By Kim Boudreau

Knowing I wanted to be an entrepreneur and having the confidence to see it through are two completely different things.

Thursday, September 2 was the day my life would boldly change, forever.

It is 7 pm, and I am finishing up a two-hour commute home. I can't believe how beautiful it is outside. The sun is shining and it's unseasonably hot for this time of year. Soon, I will be poolside with a glass of wine, enjoying the rest of the evening and sharing my day with my children and husband.

I push in the clutch and begin to apply the break, preparing to slow down as I notice the warning sign ahead. I'm relieved to be almost home. It's been a long day of work and travel.

I see several teens on the side of the highway. This is a familiar site on hot days. They are all coming out of the woods with towels wrapped around their shoulders, all tanned and glowing from the day's sun. I know where they've been all day. I know because I went there as a teen. I have been in those woods and to that beautiful white sandy beach hidden in the forest. I love that lake. Sand as far out as you can walk. So many memories!

As I watch them climb the bank and prepare to cross the four-lane highway I pull my eyes back from the teens and back to reality.

My world is about to change dramatically. I am about to take "Bold steps to a beautiful life!" Ready or not, here I come.

As I look back to the highway in front of me all I see is glowing bright red brake lights. I slam on my brakes. Too late, I was travelling too fast to stop. The noise is defining.

There are no accidents in life. I truly believe that. And looking back I believe that was my wake up call. God was saying, "HELLO! YOU'RE NOT LISTENING. I BET YOU'LL LISTEN NOW!"

Hitting a stopped vehicle, while traveling 80 kilometers an hour was not great for my car, but even worse for my body. I was so angry with myself for not paying attention. I got out of the car to find that no one was hurt, and I was relieved.

It seems an older lady also saw the teens on the side of the highway and panicked- slamming on her brakes and causing a chain reaction. How the accident happened really isn't the point. The point is, I wasn't listening...

What I didn't know yet was that this was the BEST thing that could have happened to me. My life was spinning out of control and this accident was going to bring everything to a sudden STOP!

After many years working for the same company, I decided it was time for change. Even though I enjoyed working in Jewellery and Gift, I was not feeling appreciated and knew that it was time to move on. I left my career and became a stay at home mom. After a few episodes of Barney, I quickly realized that I needed to get back into the work world.

I became a Mary Kay consultant and on to Sales Director. To supplement my income I started a little business on the side doing graphic designer work for direct sales companies throughout Canada. It was around this time that I set up a room in my home as Kreative Design, a little boutique full of handbags and accessories for women. And, if that wasn't enough, I was also holding down a part time job as a housekeeper, and traveling to do jewellery repairs. Yes, I was working five part time jobs and trying to raise a family.

A typical day began at 6 am and ended late in the evening. I would go to my cleaning job from 8 am till noon. Before I would leave, I'd change in the bathroom into a business suit and become a Mary Kay Sales Director all afternoon and some evenings. When I wasn't doing Mary Kay I was working on my graphic design business or the jewellery repair business. Plus, a few hours a week I would set times for ladies to drop in to shop at our Kreative Design boutique.

MY LIFE WAS CRAZY! And beginning to spin out of control.

Then, the accident happened.

I took that weekend to try to heal my body, but by Monday I felt even worse. Every muscle was screaming. I went back to work, but after a few days of agony I knew I needed to take time off.

I was in a panic. What would I do if I couldn't work? How could I afford time off?

I knew I could not do physical labor, so I took sick leave from my cleaning job. The graphic business was the next to go. I could not sit at the computer for long periods of time because of the pain in my neck and back. I was realizing that things had to change.

Maybe this was the perfect opportunity to really concentrate on growing my Kreative Design Business. If I could work the business and get it to the point where it would replace my cleaning income, I would not go back to the cleaning job. Could I do it? I remember sitting and talking it over with my husband. He asked me, "Are you sure you can make money selling purses and jewellery?" This unbelievable feeling of calm took over, and I said, "I know I can make money selling purses and jewellery!"

The decision was made. We turned the top floor of our home into a boutique and from 10 am to 6 pm every day, our home was a business. I created a Facebook Fan page and began promoting the business. Quickly word got out and before long there were lineups at the door.

Our mission was simple. Bring in unique high fashion products from all over the world, keep our quantities limited and give our clients a feeling of exclusivity. We branded our products as K. D. X. X for X-clusively For You. And women loved it!!

I remember my AHA Oprah Moment. I had just flipped the sign to CLOSED on another busy day in our little boutique. Our little business was not only replacing my income from the cleaning job, but also from the marketing work and my Mary Kay Director income. I said to my husband, "What took me so long! Why did it take me this long to figure out what I've known my whole life?"

It seems so clear now. I know that owning and operating my own business is what I was always meant to do with my life. But it took a car accident for me to take the bold steps to make it a reality.

I still have some pain from the accident. The aches and pains serve as a reminder to keep listening to my inner voice. Pay attention. Trust my instincts.

So here I am, three and a half years in business with so much to be grateful for. We have evolved beyond our home and into a beautiful boutique in a strip mall. We now carry K. D. X. clothing, as well as the handbags and accessories that we started with.

Being bold is scary! Deciding to become an entrepreneur is scary! Listening to your inner voice is life altering.

Of course there are sleepless nights and worries. That is part of being in business. But I am finally doing what I was meant to do. Confidently, taking bold steps to a beautiful life.

JENNY DUMONT

Jenny is a native California girl and now a Michigander with the love her life Mike and her daughter Emma Grace. Her 20-year-old son now lives in Colorado. She is a business owner of Referral Institute Mid Michigan. She is the lifeline for businesses who struggle to generate consistent, proactive referrals to live their happily ever after life. Her passion and stubbornness are trademarks in her training and coaching of referral marketing.

Jenny is an avid golfer, which is how she met Mike. Together they love to travel and experience music, theatre and good wines.

A Place for Grace is grounded in Saginaw, Michigan, and will be expanding throughout Michigan in the future. It is a childcare facility that will offer after school and summer care for children with special needs.

🏠 **Connect with Jenny and links to her resources at www.jennydumont.com**

✉ jennyd@referralinstitutesaginaw.com

📞 **(989) 714 9531**

CHAPTER 20

MY ONGOING BUTTERFLY EFFECT

By Jenny Dumont

I can't believe how many people showed up! A Place for Grace is really opening and everyone that supported us and believed in what we are doing showed up! So many lives are going to be changed by making this happen, including my Emma Grace's life. The building is perfect; we have all the education and adaptive tools we need to make sure every child with special needs feels comfortable, safe, has fun, plays, learns, grows, and, most of all, gives their parents peace of mind. It is perfect, and A Place for Grace is going to change the lives of each child, each parent, each family that it was created for!

That is my dream that I continue to replay in my head since I made the decision to start A Place for Grace. It was really only for my daughter, Emma Grace. I want a place for her to go after school and summers where I know she is safe and taken care of the way she NEEDS to be taken care of. That afternoon sitting in the parking lot of her daycare, having just picked her up for the fourth time that week because she had a meltdown, was a defining moment. It was at that point that my newest butterfly effect happened! Walking into the daycare seeing my daughter crying without emotion in her eyes, being held by a caregiver to keep her from hitting her head on the wall, or hitting other caregivers, was it! They tried to protect her to the best of their ability. It wasn't their fault, but that is all they knew what to do. My instincts kicked in and A Place for Grace was formed.

It will change the lives of many families with children with special needs across the world. This isn't the only butterfly effect that I have experienced. Each decision I made for as long as I can remember has changed lives! Not only mine, but the people around me – my brothers, my sons, my mothers, my ex-husbands and of course, my Emma Grace. Some were not always for the best, but they changed lives.

I think it might be important to help you understand a little about the butterfly effect concept. The butterfly effect is a term used in chaos <u>theory</u> to describe how small changes to a seemingly unrelated thing or condition can affect large systems. The term comes from the suggestion that the flapping of a butterfly's wings in South America could affect the weather in Texas, meaning that the tiniest influence on one part of a system can have a huge effect on another part.

How does the saying go, if you don't know where to start, start from the beginning, or at least from when you can remember. In each of our lives, there are situations that happen that you don't realize are going to make such a dramatic effect later in life, and that is exactly what I thought growing up. Who would have known that being such a stubborn young lady (as my Nana used to call me) was actually a blessing?

My story probably isn't much different from many others, but it is mine.

The earliest I can remember was when I was about 11 years old and my family just moved to a small central coast town in California called Paso Robles from southern California. We moved around quite a bit before we settled in Paso. My mom had already divorced her second husband Larry. My sister and I were from her first marriage and then my little brother was from her second. Larry adopted my sister and I when we were very young, so to me, he was my dad until I was told differently after he passed away when I was 13.

Once we were settled in Paso, my mother met a man. Personally, I wouldn't call him that, because a real man would not treat people the way he did. I have some choice names I used to call him, and I really don't even like saying his name, so for the purposes of this story – we will just call him Chip. He used to eat potato chips with ketchup – weird!

Chip was a bully in every sense of the word! Living with a bully is a lot different then just going to school with a bully. In fact, I preferred being at school or other friends' houses more then being home. Chip was a physically, emotionally, and verbally abusive man. He wasn't discriminatory to who was on the other end of it either. However, there was something inside me that was a like a switch when it came to dealing with him. I didn't show him fear! And he knew it. I was stubborn and opinionated. Making that decision not to let this so called man take control of my emotions was a decision I am glad that I made.

I used that stubbornness to protect my younger brother. He was such a boy! My brother is five years younger than me, and has always been a little shorter. He was sure a cutie too. As boys go, he was a boy. Unfortunately, he never had a good father figure around except our uncles. Thank goodness for our family. At least we had some good male role models around us. My brother (who I am intentionally keeping nameless) got into things and was curious and fun. We used to climb trees together all the time and plot our revenge on Chip. Where we lived was in close proximity to a riverbed. We would go out and explore all the time. Behind us was a ranch with a huge hill and a water tank. We used to climb the hill, catch rabbits in the irrigation pipes, explore the water tank and roll down the hill. We sure did have some fun memories! It even snowed once and we used trash bags wrapped over cardboard to go sledding down the big hill.

Unfortunately, those good memories are overshadowed by bad ones. There were many times that I had to protect my brother from Chip because no one else did. My older sister was able to move out of the house early, so I was my brother's only defense. There are many stories, some that I can't bear to write. Many of my memories involved me standing in the corner of our kitchen, with my brother behind me. I was holding a large kitchen knife telling Chip that if he came any closer I would stab him. And I meant it! You better believe it. I was the one who would pull Chip off my brother when he pushed him to the ground in his bedroom putting weight on his chest to the point he couldn't breathe. Of course, he turned his rage on me and pushed me up against the wall and cocked his fist. I can even hear my voice like it was yesterday saying, "go ahead," and he punched the wall next to me.

I was fortunate in one aspect; because our house had only two bedrooms, my sister and I (before she moved out) shared a "room" that actually was a small trailer on our property. I could "escape" to my room when I had enough. It used to be my grandpa's, but we got the trailer when he moved into a small apartment behind my aunt's home in town.

Another place my brother and I would escape to was a tree on our property. This was no ordinary tree. It was a low growing tree that draped over itself, almost like a weeping willow. We could hide inside the tree, under the branches. We spent the night there several times because it was cool! It also had access to a phone jack. Remember those? I am not sure why that tree had a phone jack in it, but it was used many times to call for someone to pick us up because we were running away. My mother and Chip wouldn't be able to stop us from calling someone because they didn't know! I had a friend that lived about a half a mile away, and I would walk there sometimes. Of course, we ended up having to return at some point.

I know that if I hadn't made the decision to protect my brother as much as I could, he would turn out the same way and continue the pattern. We hear that all the time. How many of us have heard the stories that because a child was abused, he then becomes an abuser? My brother is absolutely NOT an abuser. He is an amazing Christian MAN who loves and adores his beautiful wife and three precious children. I love the man that he has become, and I am so unbelievably proud of him. I know that he will never be like Chip. I truly believe that because of my support, protection and stubbornness, his path was changed! I carry those emotions and memories with me and use them to support and be stubborn in everything I do.

When I hear of stories from family members about abuse, I know exactly how hard it is to come forward and speak about it. I wish I would have, but I felt like if I did, I would lose my mother and I felt like I needed to protect her too. That was the only way I knew how.

My story of plain ole' stubbornness isn't the only example of how the slight shift of my actions changed the future of something greater. Moving to Michigan 13 years ago was a decision that has created challenges with my relationship with my son, whom I dearly miss. I

also gave birth to Emma Grace, who is changing the future of many –
and all of this stemmed from stretching my own wings to be a lifeline
for my brother. It is deeply rooted in why I do everything I do.

What is your ongoing butterfly effect? Maybe it hasn't started yet.
Maybe it is time! I am not done yet!

JILL HAAS

Jill Haas is a holistic nurse, spiritual intuitive healer and licensed Heal Your® Life Coach. She coaches women and teens by inspiring them to look deeper within and love who they see. Her programs create space for awareness, enlightenment and personal transformation. She mentors teens for Reaching Higher and passionately empowers young people to be happy. When she's not working, you'll find her outside playing with her dogs, doing yoga, meditation or listening to music, which she feels is a total mood changer. If you're in the Howell area, she'd be delighted to join you for an almond milk latte.

✉ jill@infinitehappyness.com

⌂ www.infinitehappyness.com

Q+ www.google.com/+JillHaas

f www.facebook.com/infinitehappyness.com

f www.facebook.com/jillmhaasrn

🐦 www.twitter.com/coachjillhaas

ⓟ www.pinterest.com/jillmhaas

in www.linkedin.com/pub/jill-haas/10/116/471

CHAPTER 21

THREE SECRET LITTLE WORDS

By Jill Haas

"If you want to keep a secret, you must also hide it from yourself."

– George Orwell, 1984

We are all beings worthy of love, and I believe love is the key to really living our lives fully and completely. Often times I notice it missing in others' lives. I'm not saying this is lacking in my life, at least not anymore. And I am not talking about romantic love.

As a little girl, the *feeling* of love was something I knew I had felt many times without being self-conscious, although the word "love" wasn't necessarily attached to the feeling yet. It was a warm and genuine feeling that flowed through me. It made me smile. Sharing the feeling with others seemed natural and inviting even if I would only intend sharing it from a distance. Fear wasn't in the equation. I willingly embraced it. It was an unconditional emotion for me. This is how we are all born into this world and somehow it changed for some of us, including me.

Growing up, I loved my parents, and I *felt* they loved me. However, the expression "I love you" was not verbalized often within our family as a whole, including relatives. These words didn't come up, at least not in my memory. The phrase seemed to be secret and private. Memories of my dad saying he loved me are non-existent. Maybe he did, but I just don't recall. One year on my birthday I do remember him leaving a voice mail message for me. His exact words escape me, but it was something like, "I remember the day you were born being a very important day in my life." I appreciated hearing this because I knew it was my dad's way of showing his love for me without saying those three little words.

I recall one very vivid moment of few, when my mom said those three words. In my early 30's, I was heading to the hospital to be admitted for complications with a molar pregnancy. I had just had an outpatient D&C and was hemorrhaging. After contacting the doctor on call, orders were to go under observation, and I called to let her know. Out of the blue, I remember her blurting out in a fearful and rather shaky voice *"I love you!"* She was obviously worried and wanted to be sure I heard this in the event something unexpected happened. It was understandable and I'll be honest, it felt odd. I have no doubt she meant it, however hearing those words were not the norm.

I imagine the pattern started somewhere back in time and was carried on from parent to child over and over again in the history of our family. I don't blame my parents, their parents or anyone for that matter. I realize this was something they too experienced. Everyone was playing out what they learned, and it's just the way it was. After hearing stories of my dad's parents, I can guess that these three little words were not spoken and if anything, maybe quite the opposite was verbalized. My mom has shared that when she was a child, the relationship with her parents was not exactly warm either.

I have been witness to the phrase "I love you" passed from people's lips as if on autopilot. Words tossed back and forth just as the simple expressions, "Hello, goodbye and thank you." In fact, I'm suspect now to some of those spoken words being born more out of habit than feeling. They lack sincerity and seemed hollow.

Discomfort churned within me when I'd hear a classmate's parent expressing these words in public or vice versa. When I heard them aloud, it gave me a funny feeling inside. I was embarrassed for them. Since we didn't say it freely and openly at home, it seemed like something to keep private and not mention in front of others, almost taboo.

"If I know what love is, it is because of you."

– Hermann Hesse

In grade school, the feelings I had for boys were considered "puppy love," or at least that is how it was explained to me. Merriam-Webster defines this as "romantic love that is felt by a child or teenager and that is not considered by adults to be real love." My grandmother made it clear I didn't know what I felt. I was told my feelings were cute and silly because I was too young to know. The sad truth of it is I did know what I was feeling. I allowed people to talk me out of it, only because I didn't know any better. I believed what I was taught and learned not to question adults. Hence, I learned not to feel anymore and to wait for someone to tell me when love was real for me. I shut off my own inner guidance. According to them my feelings were not accurate, or so I thought.

Around age ten, I noticed times when I felt the urge to tell someone "I love you," my throat would clamp down while embarrassment ensued. My heart would race, butterflies would flutter in my belly and my face would flush to a scarlet hue. And if that didn't clue the person in on how I was feeling with my "secret" emotion, I don't know what would. I just could not say it! Finding the courage to say these secret little words was challenging to say the least. It was as if by saying these words I was letting others know I was from another planet. The strong feeling of being judged overrode the ability to express love verbally.

"Love is the great miracle cure. Loving ourselves works
miracles in our lives."

– Louise L. Hay

I was losing the connection with myself, which disconnected me from others. It shouldn't be a surprise that I started to dislike myself. Eventually dislike turned to hate since I had cut myself off from feeling love. That is really what caused me to choke on my words. How could I feel it for others if I could not feel it for myself? The genuine love I felt for others dissipated after letting go of trusting my own feelings and instead allowing others to tell me how I *should* feel about them.

In order to find my connection again, I started on an inadvertent journey of self-discovery. In my teens I disliked people in general as a result of not liking myself. I didn't trust people or their intentions. Words of "like" and "love" were empty to me due to my mistrust. Oddly enough, even though most people annoyed me, it became evident that I was looking for people to validate me as being loveable and worthy of love because I truly didn't love me. Regardless, I continued to risk trusting others in different types of relationships because I really wanted to *feel* love again. I wanted to trust it was real, and I longed for that connection with friends, boyfriends and family. The love was there all along, although I didn't remember. Oblivious, I was totally disconnected from it and didn't recognize it.

My efforts proved to be pointless. I had lost touch with the loving feeling that used to live inside of me. I went through many character-building moments that directed me toward learning to love myself again. This journey carried on through my teens, twenties and thirties. Through relationship trial, error, forgiveness and acceptance, I was able to appreciate and love *me* again. I started to feel that connection with myself and people. I released judgments of myself and others, which kept me from fully connecting. Finally, I was beginning to feel love as I did before!

Loving me again has changed my life. Now I am doing what I did as a child, feeling and beaming love to others unbeknownst to them, either in direct conversation or from a distance. Additionally, I feel freer than ever to say those three little words, "I love you!" It's completely natural. I know I feel it now and alive inside of me without the need for validation from anyone!

Loving yourself may seem **BOLD** to some, but it is this love that truly makes you beautiful. I invite you to connect with and feel the love inside of you. Share it with the world the best way you know how. Most of all, I encourage you to love yourself.

I know I am not alone in my experience. Sharing my short story of love with you may be a bold move because yes, my parents are still alive and well. Even though I know all that I know now and experienced my life the way I did, it's not their fault and I would not change a thing. I love them dearly. These three little words are no longer a secret and are meant to be shared:

I love you!

References:

Puppy Love [Def. 1]. (n.d.). Merriam-Webster Online. In Merriam-Webster. Retrieved October 29, 2013, from http://www.merriam-webster.com/dictionary/puppy%20love.

THERESE SKELLY

Therese Skelly works with heart-centered entrepreneurs who love what they do and are ready to grow their businesses in a much easier and more authentic way.

She blends her background as a psychotherapist, strategist, and business consultant, and masterfully works both the inner game challenges and the outer game tactics.

From newer business owners who want to design a business that serves their life, to the already successful entrepreneurs who want to leverage their time and grow their income, Therese works with individuals like you who have a big desire to make a difference in the world. For a free gift so you can own your brilliance in your business, go to: www.Happyinbusiness.com/innermarketingebook

🏠 **www.HappyinBusiness.com**

f **www.facebook.com/therese.skelly**

f **www.facebook.com/happyinbiz**

🐦 **www.twitter.com/thereseskelly**

CHAPTER 22

HOW TO GET YOUR BRILLIANCE OUT OF YOUR BLIND SPOT AND INTO THE WORLD BY BEING BOLD

By Therese Skelly

In my mind, there's nothing worse than the pain of untapped potential. You may know that pain. It's where you sit frustrated, day after day because you know that you are capable of so much more than you are currently doing.

It can lead to feeling overwhelmed and self-doubt because after all… you have a calling, right? A soul's purpose that you said yes to. But try as you might, you cannot get that out in a way that would make you happy and profitable.

That was my story.

I was a psychotherapist, then life coach. Never did I imagine "The Dream" would take effect and I'd get a sense of the great work I was to do. So when I was guided to the world of business coaching, I said yes to that direction, but had no idea what that really meant.

Here I was with absolutely zero training in the business world. I had an undergraduate degree in criminal justice, a master's in counseling, and had worked with addicts, fighting couples, crazy inmates, and all sorts of emotional disorders, but NEVER a business owner on growing their business.

Yet I was being guided to apply for a position of business coach. It was absolutely insane on paper, but since the nudge was so strong to do it, I followed and this one decision changed the trajectory of my life forever.

I discovered that the best way for me to be of the most service in my new business was to do the inner work I needed to do to be as bold as possible. Initially, I thought it was just about learning how to grow and market businesses. It seemed like once I mastered the "outer game" skills, I'd be super successful. I was in for a huge surprise!

After a while I did get very good at the business building tactics, but I wasn't able to bring clients in as fast as I wanted. I couldn't charge what I was worth to make a good living, and secretly I was hiding out.

You see, I knew very early on that my #1 love is transformation. But I didn't own that. I was masquerading as a marketing coach. I'd tell you all sorts of ways to market your business, but I wasn't being bold in who I really was, what I really desired, or how I wanted to serve.

Until the intervention happened.

Seriously. For me it took an intervention from a group of my trusted business mastermind friends. We'd all congregated to work on our businesses and when it was my turn, they busted me. I had anticipated that they would give me business building, money making ideas.

What they did do was call me out.

I remember the words like they were yesterday. One (very bold) woman said, "Look, you are okay as a marketer, but you are brilliant with the mindset/inner game work you do. Stop hiding out. There is no one better at this work than you are, but you are not showing that to the world. No wonder your business isn't working. It's because you are not living your purpose, and you are actually selling the wrong thing. Stop it. Get your work out there. Take a stand for yourself and claim your expertise."

I have to say that this was very, very painful to hear. Why? Because I was terrified of being known as something other than a marketing coach. Thoughts ran through my head like, "No one will pay for this. How would I sell it? How do I talk about it? Who am I to do this work?"

But I knew I had to act. I could not deny the work I was supposed to share. No longer did I want to attract clients that didn't make my heart sing or who weren't the best fit. And mostly, I was no longer willing to hide my gifts.

So I just started. One small step at a time. It took tremendous courage and lots of rebranding and repositioning to get me to this place. Today, I teach my clients how to live boldly and put themselves fully into their business. I am blessed with getting to do the deep transformational work I love, with the fun, inventive business strategy piece that also feeds my creative side. It was a long journey, but today, I'm able to be very bold, fully self-expressed, and my work is branded, well known, and integrated into all that I do.

I see those years of confusion and feeling lost as a huge blessing, because now I can shortcut them for my clients. They come to me with wonderful dreams and desires and a sense for what they are supposed to be doing. Usually they are not giving themselves the permission to fully succeed making money by using all their gifts. They have the same doubts and fears, but I am that stand for them. I see myself as the "midwife for their magnificence" and delight in getting to see the results of the work all the time.

So if you are in the same place, let me share some tips for how to make sure you get your brilliance out of your blind spot and into your "profit spot" by being bolder.

The foundation for all the coaching I do comes out of my B.O.L.D.™ Business Growth Formula. This blends both the inner game (mindset) with the outer game (business strategy) that when combined, create much more rapid and lasting results because it takes into account YOU and your business. Remember – as the owner, you are the business!

Let me share with you the elements of this powerful way of looking at business:

B: BLAST IT! We blast through the blocks, belief and barriers that are in your way

O: OWN IT! Own your unique vision, talent and style

L: LEVERAGE IT! Your time, talent and team

D: DESIGN IT! To serve your life, your clients, and your legacy

Too often we go into business thinking we have to be a certain way, or let go of some of the unique, fun, or quirkier parts of our personality to be "professional." The things we did or loved in the past seem to get left at the door when we don the title of "Business Owner." And yet it's these very things that when integrated, will give you far more passion and serve to attract the exact ideal clients that you'd love to work with.

Ask yourself these questions to see if you are stuck anywhere in this piece of the process:

In the area of vision – is it yours or are you living someone else's dream for you?

When we look at talent – do you really embrace and promote the expert that you are?

And for unique style – are you showing up and expressing yourself fully?

Now let me share with you some of the signs that you haven't fully owned your brilliance. You will experience procrastination, doubt, fear and indecision, do inconsistent marketing, lack a clear message (so you won't be getting referrals or be seen as an expert), and you won't be charging what you are worth. The cost is really quite high on so many levels if you think about it!

So how about if I give you a few pointers for how to begin to "OWN" what makes you magic?

First, if you were 25% more bold in expressing who you are, what would you do differently? Deep inside you is a part that would do more, speak up more, write more, and be more fully and uniquely you.

Just make the commitment to do it. Get support if you need to, but make a plan and put yourself out there a bit more to see what happens.

Next, take a look at what are you afraid of if you do show up more boldly or more with your personality shining through? For most clients I work with it's the fear that it won't appear professional enough or there will be some judgment somewhere along the way.

Leaning into some of those fears gives you freedom to enjoy your life more every day.

And finally, remember that growing a business and marketing are just opening new relationships. I liken it to dating in that if you reveal only little aspects of yourself and attempt to put on a façade, you will either attract no one, or worse yet, the complete wrong person. While it takes some courage to be BOLD in your business, the more you put yourself out there, the greater the changes that your perfect "tribe" will find you!

The world needs you. We need your gifts and perspective. Mostly, we need you to be as bold as you can be!

Peace!

CINDY NUNNERY

My passion is to inspire, motivate and energize people. I am committed to improving the quality of people's lives through education about health, entrepreneurship, finances and personal development. I am passionate about helping people become more energized in their lives and to be their most powerful and best versions of themselves. I'm dedicated to becoming better every day and helping others do the same – one step at a time.

Cindy has been an entrepreneur most of her life, most recently in health and wellness serving others for over 10+ years. Cindy is a Board Certified Holistic Health Coach AADP CHHC, IAHC, a graduate of the Institute of Integrative Nutrition, and a Sanoviv Health Advisor. Her philosophy isn't just about eating well and being healthy, it's about all aspects of our lives that make us human – relationships, career, finances, spirituality and more.

It is about how **to BE Happy | Healthy | Energized EVERYDAY™**.

✉ **cindy@cindynunnery.com**

⌂ **www.cindynunnery.com**

f **Join My Facebook Community: facebook.com/poweredbynutrition**

f **Connect with me personally: facebook.com/cindynunnery**

🐦 **www.twitter.com/cindynunnery**

www.linkedin.com/in/cindynunnery

Skype: CindyNunnery

CHAPTER 23

BE HAPPY | HEALTHY | ENERGIZED EVERYDAY™

By Cindy Nunnery

"Just as food is needed for the body, love is needed for the soul."

– OSHO

Life is an amazing treat filled with deliciously good feelings, as well as the not so tasty ones that can come from challenges or truths that push us to the edge. Life is about being whole and courageous; happy and energized; being the student and the teacher; climbing up and falling down. It is about all the journeys along the way. It is about being beautifully bold in living and loving life.

We have but one life and each day we can choose how we want to live it, who we are going to be and what we want to feel (not how but what; more on that below).

Throughout this chapter you will see *displays of boldness,* but take them as they are meant to be – as empowerment, guidance and a little push with lots of love to help you take that step forward in being the best version of you.

[*My first display of boldness.*] I ask you to read this chapter if…

• You are ready to really FEEL Great.

• You want to be the BEST version of YOU.

- You truly desire a LIFE YOU LOVE.

- You are ready to take some steps to living your life full on.

I ask that you NOT read this chapter if:

- Passion and energy are things you run from.

- You're looking for a quick fix to anything.

- You don't want to make simple changes in your life to be your best you.

You are reading on. Awesome!

I am *deeply honored* to be part of this book and *especially happy* that you have chosen to read my chapter.

"If it looks good, you'll see it. If it sounds good, you'll hear it.
If it's marketed right, you'll buy it. But if it's true, you'll feel it."

– Kid Rock

FIRST THINGS FIRST

Let's take a moment to talk about why you're reading this. Something got you to buy this book and then read this chapter. Understanding it is the most powerful thing you can do because the potential to achieve your goals and desires, whatever they are, has increased greatly.

Are you here to learn to drop some pesky pounds, get motivated and inspired, clear up your skin, take some action on that business you want to open, move the one you have forward faster or even to just simply to learn how to be a better leader, mom, community member or spouse?

These are all wonderful goals, and you may see some of these results just by going through it. But I am going to say [*my second display of boldness.*] you're WRONG. There is another big reason why. And this is the cherry-on-top of your reason.

You want to feel a certain way!

OUR GUIDING LIGHT

Our desires, our wants and how we want to feel drive the decisions we make every day. Once we figure out how we want to feel, the rest seems to become a ripple effect in our lives moving us forward, inspiring us to keep going.

"If you begin to understand what you are without trying to change it, then what you are undergoes transformation."

– J. Krishnamutri

Have you ever given up of something before you even started it? Have you ever turned and walked away from a meeting or person you were going to meet? Have you sabotaged your own health with justifications for your lifestyle or weight issues? Have you ever felt overwhelmed at the magnitude of your goals and dreams? Do you believe they won't come true? How does this feel? Kind of deflating, doesn't it? Definitely not empowering or inspiring.

Take a moment and think of a goal you have. [*My third display of boldness.*] Don't cheat yourself by not doing this. Start writing. I promise it will be worth it.

Think about a goal you have. Do you want to kiss your spouse under the Eiffel Tower in Paris? Do you want to write a book? Start a business or change careers? Do you want to start a blog? Do you want to lose those pesky pounds, get healthier or both? Whatever it is, write it down on a piece of paper or in a journal. Be clear on your goal.

Now under that goal start to put some feelings you associate with achieving that goal. Just write them down. Will it make you feel good, powerful, connected, free, calm, authentic, vibrant, cheerful, at peace, like a leader, like a steady follower, fulfilled, strong, smart, savvy, unstoppable, loved, spiritual (any positive feeling works!)?

Can you feel it – the energy, the joy, the power as you think and write? Are you taken aback? Do you want to jump from your seat and do something – now (or stop doing something because it isn't a good thing)? As I write this chapter, I can feel what I associated with it when it was just a goal written down not that long ago. It's the excitement of making a difference. Yes, my heart is beating a little faster and it feels good. I feel alive.

And this is what it's all about. It is what we can have everyday – the awesome and wonderful feelings that go along with our greatest desires. This is what moves us into action and helps us stay focused on being the best versions of ourselves.

"The essence of your desire is a feeling. Knowing how you actually want to feel is the most potent form of clarity that you have. Generating those feelings is the most powerful creative thing you can do with your life."

– Danielle LaPorte

I am going to end with my manifesto. A manifesto is a published declaration of the intentions, motives, or views. This manifesto was written by Holstee, although I have adopted it as my own. This manifesto moves me - greatly. I have the desire to do something. I feel empowered, inspired, and, at the same time, I feel like purposeful, like a heart-centered leader. I feel guided and like the guide at the same time. I feel so much, and it is powerful. And I want this for you too. [*This is my last display of boldness*]

I URGE you to adopt this manifesto as your own, especially if your heart starts racing a little as you read it, you feel invigorated, you feel vibrant, you get excited or you even get a little sad feeling like you are withholding. Any feeling you have means there is so much more inside you waiting to get out, to make a difference, to live life to its fullest; so please, DON'T HOLD IT BACK – someone, many actually, are out there waiting to get what you have to offer. The rock star you is waiting to be let go.

Holstee Manifesto

THIS IS YOUR LIFE! Do what you love and do it often. If you don't like something, CHANGE IT. If you don't like your job, QUIT! If you don't have enough time, stop watching TV. If you are looking for the love of your life, stop. They will be waiting for you when you start doing the things that you love. Stop over analyzing, all emotions are beautiful. *LIFE IS SIMPLE*. When you eat, appreciate every last bite. Open your mind, arms and heart to new things, and people, we are united by our differences. Ask the next person you see what their passion is, and share your inspiring dream with them. *TRAVEL OFTEN*. Getting lost will help you find yourself. Some opportunities only come once...seize them. Life is about the people you meet, and the things you create with them. So go out and start creating. *LIFE IS SHORT.* Be Happy. Eat Healthy. Live your DREAM and wear your PASSION!

I love my adopted manifesto, I really do. So in closing I ask that you Be Everyday™ – be what makes you, you.

Be Loving
Be Creative
Be Genuine
Be Encouraging
Be Passionate
Be Hopeful
Be Happy
Be Healthy
Be Energized
Be Alive
Be Bold

Every day.

Here's to you!

161

BOLD IS BEAUTIFUL

DR. ANITA M. JACKSON

Dr. Anita M. Jackson is the Founder and CEO of The I Am Enough Institute and the Divas for Success Training Program. Her passion, mission, and purpose is to empower all women to know they are enough and can become outrageously successful in their personal life and business. With 24 years of experience as a psychotherapist and organizational psychologist, Dr. Anita empowers her audience to deeply and profoundly reach their highest and fullest potential in order to bring about a higher level of spiritual healing, restoration, balance and harmony to individuals, families and the world.

ADMINISTRATIVE POSITIONS

Founder and CEO, The I Am Enough Institute:

⌂ **www.iamenoughinstitute.com**

Divas for Success Training Program:

⌂ **www.theiamenoughinstitute.memberlodge.org**

SOCIAL MEDIA LINKS:

f Personal Facebook: www.facebook.com/anita.m.jackson.3

f The I Am Enough Institute Facebook:
www.facebook.com/The-I-Am-Enough-Institute

- www.pinterest.com/sljackson2911/boards
- www.linkedin.com/pub/anita-m-jackson-ed-d/2/585/180
- www.twitter.com/yesiamenough

CHAPTER 24

ℬOLDLY DECLARING I AM ENOUGH

By Dr. Anita M. Jackson

Beloved sister, I have a confession to make, and it is my hope that in my willingness to expose myself to you, dear one, you will do the same. Want to know my confession? Well, for the past 46 years of my life I have been wearing a mask. This mask, on the outside, is stunning, elegant, well put together, strong, durable, dependable and even attractive; able to distract anyone from what hides behind it. For what is behind this mask is not necessarily ugly. In truth, what is behind the mask is absolutely beautiful, radiant, strong, desirable, resilient, courageous, spiritual, divine, intuitive and all the feminine aspects and traits of God, the divine. What is even more amazing about this mask is that it is not only my mask but the mask of every woman who has unconsciously allowed the subtle effect of disappointments, hurts, pains, and fears to diminish her true brilliance and essence as a woman.

It is this mask that has indirectly caused the feminine energy and power of women to be lessened. It is this mask that has caused many women to question and doubt their own self-worth and value. It is this mask that prevents women from making even more of a contribution locally, nationally and globally. Despite all the progress women have made throughout history, there is still so much more for us to do. It is my firm belief sister, that when a woman decides to boldly remove her mask and allow herself to *truly* be seen and experienced, she boldly declares, **"I Am Enough."** It is in this bold declaration of **"I Am Enough"** that she opens herself up to a greater capacity of experiencing and serving more in her personal life as well as in her business.

MY MASK

In 2011, my mask was unexpectedly removed. After working as a psychotherapist for 24 years, and as an organizational psychologist for eight years, my body, soul and spirit had declared, "enough is enough." It was in this "unconscious" declaration that set everything in motion for me to eventually lose my job, my brand new home, the man I thought I loved, and everything else that I believed made for a "good life." Externally, I looked like I had it all together. I am tall, *6 feet*, with an attractive curvaceous figure that I am proud of. I have a charismatic personality with an infectious laugh and smile, *or so I have been told*. I am very accomplished having gone to school and graduated four times (it feels as if I have the full alphabet after my name). I modeled for a Sears catalog when I was young, participated in the development of a few well-known women's events, had the honor of meeting several well-known celebrities within personal development, honorably mentioned in two books, traveled and lived in Europe for three months, sang as back up on two gospel albums, and even participated in Disney's 25th Anniversary Celebration when I was in high school (I love knowing that I have a part in Disney's history!). I have had two very successful private practices, taught at two universities as an Assistant Professor, frequently speak at various women's events, and have been told repeatedly that I have a unique ability to empower people to their greatness whether personally or professionally. Whew, I have done a lot!

However, when all the activity of being busy, productive and accomplished ends, when the laughs and smiles fade, behind this mask of my many accomplishments was someone very different. Very few people truly knew me. Why? Because somewhere along my lifeline, I had several painful and life-altering experiences that silently and indirectly convinced me that I could never really let anyone "see" me, let alone "know" me. So, I learned very well to hide behind a mask.

During all my external successes, no one knew that my father was an alcoholic, abusive and left when I was very young. No one knew that

I struggled in school because of undiagnosed ADHD. (Now officially diagnosed, I understand my quirky personality and somewhat strange sense of humor. I now use it to my advantage because this is my greatest gift, and I know how to work it well. Yahoo!). No one knew that I struggled with severe depression for most of my young adult life because I was "holding" a deep dark secret. No one knew that I had so much self-hatred that I ate myself to 375 lbs and always thought, "…there must be something wrong with me." No one knew that I attempted suicide three times, struggled with alcoholism, and that the pain of loneliness and rejection was deathly suffocating that no amount of good deeds or prayers could quiet my internal battle. No one knew that I experienced racial discrimination that eventually caused me to be "jumped" by six girls in high school. No one knew that everything started when I was sexually abused as a child. These were my constant battles. These were my internal demons. That no matter how hard I tried, no matter how much I gave, no matter what I did or great accomplishments I made, nothing was ever good enough. And here, is where my true story begins.

Over the years, I have had the honor of working with hundreds of individuals, most of them women, who "looked" just like me; and for the first time, I finally understood the value of my experiences, my story, and my purpose here on earth. It was within the confinement of four walls and a closed door that the stories of hurting disempowered women called to me, asked questions I had asked myself for years that led me on a deep spiritual journey to find answers about worth, value, femininity, sensuality, sexuality, spirituality, self-love and self-empowerment. And boy, what a journey!

Intellectually, we all know that we should feel good about ourselves, appreciate and value our gifts, talents and abilities. We intellectually know the importance and power of "I am enough;" however many of us unfortunately struggle with our overall sense of self on a daily basis. Why? Well that would take a little more than a chapter within a book to explain; although, in simple terms it mostly has to do with never feeling good enough about who we are, what we can and are called to do, and how to go about being and living life more fully and abundantly. You see, the meaning of, "I Am Enough" is not an intellectual concept, but in fact a spiritual truth that when understood, can greatly impact our faith, energy, and vibration to such a degree that we can powerfully recreate ourselves and our lives.

Unfortunately, we are bombarded with direct and indirect social messages every day telling us that something is wrong in the way we look, in what we have or don't have, in who we are or not, and in what we are doing or not doing. The list is endless. Subconsciously, we have quietly bought into these lies causing a deep sense of soul and spiritual dissatisfaction and unrest with who we are and the life we are now living. This unrest is causing havoc on our marriages, families, mental health, physical health and social economy. It is lowering our ethics and morals. It is giving rise to more anger and hostility. Yet, on a positive note, this soul and spiritual dissatisfaction and unrest is also becoming our awakening to "get back to the basics," the truth in knowing what is and has always been true – our divinity, our likeness to and with God that, as David J. Walker says in his book, "You Are Enough"…You Always Have Been….You Always Will Be!

FOUR FOUNDATIONAL PRINCIPLES OF "I AM ENOUGH"

So, what does "I Am Enough" truly mean?

To fully understand and internalize the power of "I Am Enough," I would need to not only share the four foundational principles of "I Am Enough", which you will read here, but I would also need to share the eight specific guideposts. However, understanding the following foundational principles will powerfully enable you begin to heal and transform your life and your experiences.

First, the words "I Am" are probably two of the most powerful words a woman can utter to herself and to the universe because everything stated behind these words, whether positive or negative, becomes reality, our truth.

So, here are a few principles about **I Am Enough**.

Principle Number One – boldly declaring **I Am Enough** means you acknowledge your divinity, your creation and connection to God. This is the difference between having an awareness of God and knowing

God. In this declaration, you strengthen your internal Goddess, intuition and wisdom in such a way that you can begin to work smart rather than hard.

Principle Number Two – boldly declaring **I Am Enough** means that every experience you have had, whether good, bad or ugly, has value and importance in the development of your existence and the revealing of your higher spiritual self. If we allow this to be true, then everything that has happened and continues to happen to us opens us up to experiencing more of life richly and abundantly. Remember, however, that the opposite is just as true. If we declare, "I am not enough" then we are opening ourselves up to experience lack, a life of emptiness, dissatisfaction and unrest.

Principle Number Three – boldly declaring **I Am Enough** means you are stating that everything after this statement is true, "I am enough in my beliefs, thoughts, emotions, characteristics and habits." This declaration empowers your conscious awareness of who you are and how you co-create your life with God through faith and believing.

Principle Number Four – boldly declaring **I Am Enough** powerfully influences your manifestation abilities. Your level of faith and belief that you are good enough greatly shapes what you are able to manifest and experience in life. In our divinity and likeness to God, we have creative abilities that allow us to display the wondrous powers of God and the Universe.

Although there is so much more to say about boldly declaring **I Am Enough** and how it influences our ability to experience outrageous success, just knowing these basic four principles can be the catalyst to helping you step up to the next level.

Let me end with this. It is time for us as women to remove our masks, release false truths, fears and expectations, and fully "show up" even more in our feminine essence, wisdom, power, abilities, and creativity. We must show up in our commitment and dedication to our divine feminine selves, as well as recognize our place in the growth and development process of our society and economy by continuing to excel in the arena of spirituality, creativity, wealth, abundance and the advancement of business. In making such a commitment to ourselves, our families, our sisters and the world, we must, as Marianne Williamson said in her famous poem *Our Deepest Fear*, "…we are all meant to shine…to make manifest the glory of God that is within us….as we let our own light shine, we unconsciously give other people permission to do the same. As we are liberated from our own fear, our presence automatically liberates others." It is time for us as women to truly shine in our brilliance, divine creation, and feminine essence and power.

Take off your mask and boldly declare **"I Am Enough."**

ROMMY KIRBY

Rommy Kirby has been interested in fitness and nutrition for over 25 years. As a yoga teacher, yoga studio owner and holistic health coach she shares her passion for wellness to help her clients and community regain control over the their health so they can enjoy optimal wellness. If you would like to contact her, send an email to Rommy@RommyKirby.com.

Rommy Kirby, E-RYT™, CHHC, AADP

Founder and Creator, Radiant Optimal Wellness

Co-owner, My HOT YOGA Place

 www.rommykirby.com/

 www.twitter.com/RommyKirby

 www.facebook.com/rommyh

 www.facebook.com/pages/Rock-Your-Radiance-with-Rommy/114058488705817

 www.youtube.com/user/RommyKirby?feature=mhee

 www.linkedin.com/pub/rommy-kirby/34/1a4/8a1

 Skype: rommy.hussey

CHAPTER 25

OLD ENOUGH TO WANT

By Rommy Kirby

Hi Beautiful,

Do you want to change the world? Do you aspire to inspire? Do you sometimes sit with your dreams, goals and ambitions thinking that you just don't have the guts to make it happen? Does the demon of discouragement tell you that you could never in a million years write a book, build a successful business, have an epic loving relationship with your beloved, your child, or your body?

The thing is, you don't have to be super bold to live the life of vibrancy, vitality and wonder you've dreamt of for so long.

You don't have to be over the top bold like Madonna or out of the box bold like Lady Gaga.

You just have to be bold enough. That's all. Just bold enough, like allowing this next breath to be enough.

The first step in any endeavor, big or small, is to be bold enough to want.

Sounds simple right?

What if I were to ask you, "What do you want right now?" could you give me a specific answer? Can you answer that question *without thinking about anyone else, what they might think or what they might want?*

What do *you* want to eat? What movie do *you* want to see? What book do *you* want to read? What kind of love relationship do *you* want? What kind of health do *you* want to enjoy? What do *you* want to leave, begin or end? How do *you* want to feel?

It's only with a clear and specific want that you can take the next step free of fear and confusion.

You know when it's dark, the fog is dense and the road is narrow and unmarked, how your mind races with thoughts that every turn of the wheel is bringing you closer to impending doom? Like fog at night, confusion and lack of focus allow paralysis to set in and malaise to become our companion.

Being bold enough to want is like magically driving out of the fog into a clear night lit by the fullest moon, the road brilliantly lit before you. Your mind eases, your body relaxes and your heart rate returns to normal. You know where you're going. You know which direction you will take.

All you have to do is be bold enough to want so that you can take that next step. You see, dear, it isn't about taking that second, third or fourth step or even that one hundred and first step.

Because, gorgeous, it's the next step that counts the most – ALWAYS.

You just have to be bold enough to want the next step.

For a lot of us, myself included, becoming bold enough to want can be wickedly scary. Maybe you've noticed that as you grew into womanhood, adopting the roles of mother, wife, girlfriend, healer or teacher, that you seem to have forgotten the art of wanting. But beautiful soul, it is vitally important to the health of your mind, your body and your soul to remember it, embrace it, flex it and use as the tool it can be.

Think about this. If a baby were not bold enough to want to see, taste, feel and explore, they would fail to thrive. They would never lift their head, roll over, and learn to sit, crawl or put food in their mouths. They would not grow, or even think about pulling up. Nor would they take that first unsure step on legs that have yet to prove themselves. Babies come with an innate boldness to want to experience life.

Sadly, it seems many of us have forgotten that wanting is the spark that lights the fire of desire.

173

Maybe you hold a belief that wanting to be vibrant and alive and experience success in your health, relationships and careers is selfish. Or that wanting is the act of a selfish, spoiled, unconscious person. And that giving up desire is the highest and most virtuous sacrifice for the benefit of our families, friends and community.

I'll let you in on a secret.

That line of thinking is absolute crap. You know what crap thinking gets you?

Crap. Crap health, crap relationships, crap job, and a crap life.

I know. I once had the belief that wanting is selfish, childish, and even shameful and that *my* wants were second to all others. Oddly, it was a male family member that helped me to see that I had abandoned me for everyone else.

His family was visiting mine for a few days. Each day, there were outings, meals and gatherings to finalize. Everyone had an opinion about what they wanted, how they wanted it and when they wanted it to happen.

Then, this quiet fellow looked at me and asked, "what do *you* want?" I gave my standard answer, "I'm happy with whatever makes everyone else happy."

Normally, that answer got me recognition as a fabulous and gracious hostess. Not this time. He followed up with another question, "Surely, you have an opinion, something you prefer. Which restaurant do you want to go to tonight?"

Funny how simple, seemingly benign questions can rock us to the core.

I didn't have an answer. I realized could not think or feel want. I had suppressed it for too long. On that day in that moment I realized that wanting is not selfish but vital to the survival of me.

Gradually, I became aware of a lifetime of conditioned beliefs and messed up perceptions of virtue, grace, strength, honor and femininity. You see, in my culture and my family, strength meant not needing help, virtue meant sacrifice, and grace in sacrifice was honorable. To hold those beliefs means that wanting is a weakness, a vice.

But even Mother Theresa, the most notable giving selfless woman of our time wanted. She wanted to serve, ease suffering and bring peace to others. Imagine that if, as a young girl, she hadn't allowed herself to want. She would never have been bold enough to take action, giving up everything to move to India and follow her passion, her purpose. She would never have fed the hungry, nursed the sick or ennobled the outcast.

Now, changing lifelong beliefs and becoming bold enough to want to experience life doesn't happen overnight. Yes, sweet one, it can also be exquisitely scary.

Why?

Because being bold enough to want means that you are on a path. A path that leads towards the life, the love, the relationships, the body and the career you want. It means that you are ready to make a commitment to being fully you. Not the you your parents, family or your culture designed, but the you that you have dreamed of being since you were a girl.

Do you remember that girl that wanted?

There are many steps on the way to the life of your dreams. It's the next step that counts always. All you have to do is be bold enough to want to take it.

My wish for you, sweet soul, is that you can say and feel, "I Am Bold."

I Am Bold Enough to Want…
I Am Bold Enough to Want To Feel
I Am Bold Enough to Want To Do
I Am Bold Enough to Want To Go
I Am Bold Enough to Want To Get
I Am Bold Enough to Want To Have
I Am Bold Enough to Want To Release
I Am Bold Enough to Want To Live
I Am Bold Enough to Want to Be…

– *Me*

STACIE WALKER

Stacie Walker is an Online Business Strategist, Author, Online Radio Host, and the founder of the Woman in Leadership online community.

Stacie officially said goodbye to the corporate world in 2008 without regrets and has not looked back on the career she left behind.

Known as a success-driven entrepreneur, it has been Stacie's mission and purpose to educate aspiring and existing entrepreneurs to possess the correct tools to establish a better business model. She also is an ongoing student of personal development. She has combined her acquired knowledge on personal development and business advice to improve the quality of life of her clients.

A top priority of Stacie is to provide a comfortable place for the novice and the experienced entrepreneur to get a bit of inspiration, motivation, and business building strategies for long term success. She believes all of the above elements are essential to improve your skill set as a budding entrepreneur in your industry.

She has committed her life to be of service to people across the world, and believes it's crucial to provide real value, in order to create stronger businesses, communities and alliances.

⌂ www.WomanInLeadership.com

🐦 www.twitter.com/StacieWalker

f www.facebook.com/WomanInLeadership

CHAPTER 26

FROM ROCK BOTTOM TO MOVING MOUNTAINS

By Stacie Walker

It's important to realize that your negative experiences – you know, the dark places you found yourself in at some point in your life – can be of great benefit to others.

I'm talking about the rock bottom times in your life that you would rather forget. The truth is these are the experiences that you will NEVER forget. These are the types of experiences you may have not told a single soul about or have done your best to pretend that your rock bottom situations never have happened.

It's so easy to leave out key elements in our life story. I believe we do this to avoid going through those emotions all over again. Being women, those negative emotions will flood over us as if we are reliving some of the biggest nightmares of our past.

We may also leave out key elements while sharing our life story because we don't want others to judge us. Who likes to be judged? I don't, and I'm pretty sure you don't like being judged either. The people who judge you are the people who most likely need to clean up their own backyard. These are the people who will not benefit from the true message of your story.

Forget about those people because they will cause distractions and may influence you to second guess yourself. I encourage you to not back down. Your goal is to focus on the people you can help by sharing all of your experiences. Being transparent will allow you to connect with and bond with people on a deeper level. They will know that you are authentic. They will know you are human, not a robot.

Sometimes we can be deceived into thinking that the most successful people we admire do not go through setbacks, disappointments, and horrible experiences. We are deceived because we usually gather detailed information about their successes, not their failures. The good thing is that successful people from different backgrounds are breaking out of the monotony and are willing to share their entire life journey up to the present day. These are the individuals to pay attention to because they teach us that it's okay to just be ourselves.

I think we are harder on ourselves when we go through dark moments in our life. But this is the perfect time to not be difficult on yourself. Unfortunately, I have experienced several pain slashing heartbreaks that put me on the downward spiral of hitting rock bottom more than once.

I remember with great clarity how much it seemed that there was no end to the instability that I was going through in my life. I remember feeling as if this was how my life was supposed to be, full of heartache, pain, and sadness. On another note, late at night when I was resting my head, a small voice in the back of my mind spoke to me during the silence. That voice whispered that I'm not embracing how to truly live. I would then fight that small voice by cutting it off with the loud noise of negative self-talk. It was a constant battle, and it caused me great distress and unease for a long time. I knew in my heart that I was a good person and I didn't deserve to live such a pitiful life.

I'm humble enough to admit that I have had more than one "rock bottom" moment in my life; however, one life experience stands out more than the others. It is the experience that forever changed me.

I rented my first apartment when I was 19 years old. I thought life was great. I finally had a space of my own choosing for the first time in my life. Looking back, I was in no position mentally to accept that responsibility. It was a two bedroom apartment right in the middle of a growing community of college students, and I partied with fellow students from the neighborhood.

My roommate and I decided to throw a small party of about 20 people. Well, 20 people turned into over 100 people. There was obviously no room left inside my apartment, so some of the partygoers gravitated outside to the tidy, grassy lawn in front of the complex. That is when I realized that news traveled fast in that neighborhood, and that we just threw the party of the year.

College students in big numbers usually means an out of control event. The next day my landlord was disposing the trash, and discovered which tenants hosted a alcohol fueled event that practically destroyed his investment. All he had to do was follow the beer cans and cigarette butts that trailed right to my front door.

Having my first apartment lasted for about six months. Due to my irresponsibility, I was evicted, and my roommate and I went our separate ways. My parents and I were not on good terms at the time because I wasn't willing to let go of my wild lifestyle. Because of my choices and stubbornness, living with either of my parents wasn't an option.

My days of living carefree and wild ended fast. My life took a turn for the unexpected worse. I was homeless. You would think out of all the people I knew that one would have let me room with them. That's when I really found out who my friends were.

I spent a week sleeping at a well-known hotel chain located in downtown San Antonio. I didn't sleep in a room; I slept in the service stairwell. I tucked my 115 pound body behind the fire hose storage area to stay out of sight at night. Early in the morning, I ate food from the cart left by the service elevator. I managed to not be seen the entire time I stayed there.

It was sad. I remember crying at night and feeling so alone. On the eighth day, I finally begged and pleaded with my dad to let me stay with him. He agreed to take me back in. That chapter in my life ended.

What did I learn from that experience? Nothing. I moved out of my dad's house a few weeks later and continued to live a life of substance abuse and irresponsibility.

I was in my first committed relationship, and I thought it was love at first sight. I knew nothing about having a wholesome, healthy, intimate relationship with anyone. Of course, I didn't even think about my lack of relationship skills at the time. We hit it off great; so great that we ended up going to the Justice of the Peace six months later.

What a mistake! I ended up staying in an unhealthy relationship for eight years fueled by drug use and co-dependency. I knew for sure at that point in time that I never wanted to be in that situation again. I had invested a lot of time, blood, sweat, and tears into that relationship. I couldn't bear having a repeat episode with another partner. I was so heartbroken that I ended up with increased substance abuse problems, depression, and was sleeping 20 hours a day.

It was a horrible place to be in.

I never thought my heartache and pain would go away. I didn't love myself and I didn't open my heart up to healing and finding the right kind of support system.

Then it finally hit me. My life was in such a bad place that I couldn't stand living like that any longer. I made the decision to make the necessary changes to move mountains to turn my life around and properly heal.

What did I learn from that experience? I learned so much that it has forever changed me as a person. I learned what I could do to prevent that type of heartache from happening again. I also learned how to properly love myself, so that I could receive proper love from others.

My life now is fabulous! I would have never dreamed in a million years that my life could be this fantastic; and it's getting better and better as the days go by. Every area of my life is full of LOVE and SUPPORT. I will not settle for less.

This year (2013) has been the year of moving mountains in my personal life. I never thought that I would be living a fantastic and peaceful life. I'm no longer a product of my environment. My environment is a product of the things that I want in my life.

I have been able to find out more about myself, and I have discovered my purpose in life. I have been able to forgive others, but mostly, I have been able to forgive myself.

Through my experiences, good and bad, I have learned who my true friends are along the way. I have had to say goodbye to most of my old acquaintances. but I have gained new relationships through my journey as an entrepreneur. I still experience disappointments, but it's a relief to know that my dark, rock bottom days are getting further and further behind me.

I am still presented with some of the greatest challenges in my life, but I continue to press on and achieve great success and personal satisfaction. Today, I can actually say that I'm happy and mean it. I have learned to love myself. Because I have learned to love myself, I have more meaningful relationships with my family and friends. I'm so grateful to be surrounded with people that can lift me up and not bring down. It has been a long road for me, but my journey has not been for nothing. For a long time, I was clueless to what my purpose is in life.

I overcame obstacles that seemed almost impossible to conquer. I have moved mountains to get to my current level of success with my business and my life.

I urge you to let go of the past, because you can never get that time back. Let go of all of the past disappointments and losses that others may have imposed on you. Learn to let go and forgive others. What matters most is that you forgive yourself.

Experiences like these change your life!

We all have our rock bottom moments, and each of those experiences are unique and never the same. All of these moments lead to the same place, self-discovery. It's up to you what you do with these experiences. You can choose to do nothing or you can choose to move mountains, too.

SHEILAH M. WILSON

Sheilah M. Wilson is an extraordinary Success and Spiritual Coach focused on Conscious Eating, in addition to being an entrepreneur, teacher, author, and facilitator of mindfulness exercises, guided imagery and energy psychology techniques. She is a Licensed Professional Counselor, Licensed Independent Substance Counselor, certified Master Addiction Counselor, and Board Certified Coach. Sheilah has accumulated more than 13,000 hours coaching clients to achieve transformational results. She is brilliantly insightful and intuitive, respectful and compassionate. Sheilah has a diverse background of experience and expertise that grounds her in the unique position of being able to awaken, catalyze, and support those who come to her with a variety of issues, blocks, needs, concerns and goals. Sheilah works hard to be as healthy as she can be mentally, emotionally, physically and spiritually; this heart-centered commitment allows her to be the best possible coach and mentor for her clients.

⌂ **www.sheilahmwilson.com**

$\mathcal{T}$URNING OBSTACLES INTO OPPORTUNITIES

By Sheilah M. Wilson

Being bold also means being brave. Many times in my life I have had to stand alone in my truth while others nearby disagreed or disapproved. Who shall I disappoint? Myself or others? How important is it to "fit in"? How can I be of service and share my unique gifts if I deny who I am just because I don't want to hurt someone else's feelings? To be bold is to be brave and to have the courage to honor my beliefs, values, boundaries, needs, dreams, and ideals. I no longer accept less than I know myself to be, and this includes turning obstacles into opportunities.

While obstacles appeared to block my way, prevent or hinder progress, opportunities all around me provoked a set of circumstances that made it possible to do something. I choose to see the possibilities and remember that I really do have a choice in every moment. And it is all in my perspective – how I decide to view my life and understand what was happening at the time is all a matter of perception. Today, I can say, "I am a warrior, not a victim." I have practiced and internalized this belief over decades, and now it is my truth.

My life has been rattled with many, many obstacles that usually felt overwhelming and insurmountable at the time, but I practiced looking for the "gift," the lesson or opportunity to grow by challenging myself to get through the situation as best I could. Always as best I can. One of the keys that guides my way is the Serenity Prayer:

God, grant me the serenity to accept the things I cannot change,
The courage to change the things I can,
And the wisdom to know the difference.

– *Reinhold Niebuhr*

By accepting the situation, I give myself space to respond rather than remain in the trance of automatic pilot and react based on old memories, unconscious conditioning, patterns and programs. Acceptance is a process not an event, so I allow things to be as they are in order to create the opportunity to view possibilities. Allowing does not mean I agree with what is happening; fully acknowledging what is in the moment is the perfect place to start to determine what I can change and what I cannot change. The only place where one can begin to make changes is being present with what is.

NOW is the place of power. If I am whimpering about the past or freaking out about the future, I cannot change the present. And changing the present is the only way to impact the future.

Here are the six steps I follow to turn obstacles into opportunities.

1. Acknowledge what is. It might be ugly or painful, but ignoring it or pretending that it is something other than what it is does not help change the situation.

2. Allow myself to feel my emotions about the situation. I cry, I am angry, I feel hurt, I am scared, and it is all okay. I do practice avoiding blame, judgment or shaming myself about the situation. Steps 1 and 2 are part of acceptance – the only place from which I can truly change.

3. Postpone any important decisions or responses until I am more calm (usually the next day or later). I have learned to be patient with myself and give myself gentleness and time to take action. Today, I can say, "Let me get back to you with my answer" without feeling pressured to always know what to do in the moment.

4. Use my head and heart to "see, hear and feel" the possible opportunities by asking such questions as, "How can I get out of this mess?", "What do I need to do to create a positive outcome?"

or "What is the next most important thing I need to do?" I am often surprised at the answers I get to these questions, but I trust and follow my head and heart working together with integrated rational and emotional intelligence. There are no mistakes in my world, only choices.

5. Take baby steps in the direction of my needs and values, while watching and waiting for additional internal guidance along the way. I use FasterEFT to continue to clear the way of past memories, unconscious programs and unresourceful, limiting beliefs.

6. Remain "teachable" and open to continued discovery of my truth through daily quiet time (reflection, journaling, walking, and meditation).

So much of turning obstacles into opportunities is about attitude and beliefs. I can choose to be happy for no reason just because I do not want to experience this day in sadness, regret, fear or depression. This is not pretending everything is ok, but rather, it is a practice of acknowledging this day will never come again, and I want to live it to the fullest possible. It really is a choice.

When I look back on my life, I can see how amazing and magical it all has been – more beautifully orchestrated than I could have done by myself. My greatest part in all my success through adversity has been my KNOWING (beyond belief) that everything always turns out for the best. I learn and grow, and I can decide how to avoid an unpleasant experience from re-occurring by learning as much as possible about how I managed to attract the circumstance into my life in the first place. I take full responsibility for everything in my life; it is all a reflection and projection of who I think I am at the time.

At age seven, I had major surgery to remove a benign tumor from my left leg. The operation removed a chunk from my leg that gave many children reason to tease and call me unkind names. This obstacle to being accepted helped me develop a friendly and outgoing personality. Many more obstacles turned into wonderful opportunities throughout my school days. When a door closed, it was often some form of protection to keep me safe and away from unknown danger or difficulties (no more drama in my life, please!).

Professionally, I was given the opportunity to trust my values and standards by not giving into seductions and propositions to "get the order" from customers when working for IBM. I stood my ground for self-respect and was still able to meet my sales goals and be successful as a Marketing Representative without having to surrender my feminine charms.

Perhaps my greatest opportunity came during the divorce of my twenty-year marriage to an attorney. Many obstacles appeared to be keeping me from freedom, happiness and half the community property that legally was mine. But the judge disagreed, and I walked out of the marriage with only my personal items. My attorney insisted I appeal the lower court's  decision (of the violation of the community property law), but I decided I no longer wanted to be attached to a destructive relationship. I did not want to spend another $30,000, 18 months of waiting, and take the risk the tribunal would not over-turn the lower court's obviously unfair and illegal decision. This was the right decision for me, even though some disagreed.

As devastating as the divorce was emotionally, physically, psychologically, and financially, I kept my dignity and self-respect, and saw the opportunity to renew and begin my life again, one day at a time. It was difficult. After many years of serious grieving, introspection, and growing, I arose from the ashes like a phoenix to return to graduate school and become a licensed psychotherapist and successful Board Certified Coach. I did whatever it took to make my dreams come true because I finally saw I was worth it. My greatest revenge was recreating myself, becoming successful on my own, and finding great happiness, peace and joy in my life because it was MY LIFE.

While I never viewed being single as an obstacle (to being happy, for example), the opportunity to be single was a time to rethink what kind of man and marriage I wanted to create. I became clear about my needs, values and standards, and I was blessed with a relationship with my Divine Complement. This spiritual partnership has brought me many more opportunities for growth, including learning to listen deeper, acceptance of my partner's truth and limitations as he/we see them (accepting what I/we cannot change), and new knowledge and support I had not discovered or experienced before.

"Bad things" don't happen to me anymore. I see every obstacle as an opportunity to try something new or different, stretch and grow in a way I had not planned or seen before. I allow the universe to assist me by letting go of what I cannot change or control, grieving the loss of what was or will never be, and asking for help when needed.

GWENDOLYN WEIR SWINT

Gwendolyn is a Certified Life and Transformational Coach. She is the Founder of Golden Years Coaching Services and Senior Health Matters in home Medical Services. She is currently the co-author of two mentoring/inspirational books with two International Best Selling Authors.

Gwendolyn is advancing her studies at the prestigious Academy of Coaching Cognition and is also enrolled in the School of on Line Businesses Masters and WholeLife Education Program.

Gwen and granddaughter, Heather, enjoy living together in Detroit's Historic Riverfront Community. She has one daughter, Julie Nicole, and another granddaughter, Helena, residing in Hawaii.

Gwendolyn is an intuitive coach helping her clients reach their goals effortlessly. Not without work but with ease. She can be reached via of her website.

⌂ **www.gwenswint.com**

You can contact her at:

✉ **gwendolynSwint@gmail.com**

CHAPTER 28

BE BOLD, BE BEAUTIFUL, BE AUTHENTICALLY YOU

By Gwendolyn Weir Swint

Bold is to be fearless. Bold is to live your life with courage and without the consent of others. To live your life on your terms.

Be Bold.

Have you ever felt stuck? You don't necessarily hate where you are, but you don't really like the space you're in. That would be your comfort zone. Being bold means having the courage to step out of your comfort zone. It means stepping out of the box and doing things your way. It means having the courage to let go of what no longer serves you. It means you must try something new or different if you want to get yourself to the next level. It means having the courage to conquer the fear that's holding you back. It means to take one of these small but bold steps at a time.

I was stuck in an unhappy marriage for 15 years. I was in my comfort zone, but I wasn't happy. I was routinely doing the same things day after day, not raising or lowering the bar. We all do this in one form or another until we decide to do just one thing differently, and BOOM, all of a sudden our life begins to change in unexpected ways simply because we decided to make one positive change or take one small step.

As for my situation, I wanted to know who this person was that would allow herself to be mentally and physically abused for 15 years. I sincerely wanted to help her. Deciding that I wanted to get to know this seemingly helpless person (that would be me) was the best day of my life, because it was the beginning of self-love and acceptance. Often, we get so caught up doing for those around us, we forget that we require nourishment that only we can give ourselves. That's called self-empowerment. You must do this for yourself, no one can do it for you.

Making the decision to get to know who this person was that would allow this abuse was both adventurous and bold. It was also difficult at first because the last thing your mind wants to do is change. It doesn't want you to take it out of its comfort zone. This is when you will need help.

I chose to learn the art of meditation. You can chose whatever means of calming your mind that you are comfortable with. I used mediation not as a means to an end but as a way to settle the mind. I discovered that fear and calmness cannot occupy the same space at the same time. When the mind is calm, fear is not there. Fear is an illusion. Fear is a mirage. Fear is not the reality. Taking the journey within was bold because I wasn't sure of what I would find. The hunger for freedom and peace of mind outweighed any hesitation to search for answers.

Be Bold. Be Beautiful. Beauty is in the eye of the beholder, therefore you have your own unique definition of what is beautiful. For me, beautiful is having the ability and desire to reinvent myself.

Reinventing myself was a must if I was to escape personal abuse. The problem was that I was constantly hitting the brakes, putting off doing what I needed to do to free myself because I was perhaps having what I perceived as a good day. Let me assure you, putting on brakes not only stops you, it throws you back. I had to learn to make conscious decisions to move myself forward and then stick to those decisions. Putting on brakes was no longer an option.

This doesn't mean that I didn't fall off. No shame in that. Getting back up and starting over is a must whether you are reinventing yourself or not. I had to learn to ask myself, "what do you want your life to look like? What do you want your life to feel like? Am I present in this moment or am I focusing too much on the past or looking too far into the future?" One thing I have learned is you can only live in the present moment. The past has no actual existence except in memory, and the future never arrives because we are always in this present moment. So right now in this present moment is the time for you to decide that your Bold is Beautiful.

BE AUTHENTICALLY YOU

Authentic is the real deal. If you are authentic you are trustworthy and credible.

To be authentic is to be a work in progress. Now we would all like to think of ourselves as genuine, reliable and on point all the time. That's not happening with anyone. What I love about the pursuit of authenticity is that you put yourself into the arena of lifelong learning. You are seeking a whole life education, an education that is out of the box. You're now learning from the inside out where the real authentic you is to be found. Not all learning is in a text book, the text book is only a tool box for learning.

My search for authenticity started when I found myself having a baby alone. That was, of course, the wake up call for me. I was married and having our baby alone. He was on some island living it up. The marriage was over for me even though it took the next 14 years to free myself. During those years I experienced countless encounters of physical abuse. The final straw was being in a situation that I knew I wouldn't survive unless there was going to be a miracle. The miracle happened and I was set free from that day forward. The fear dropped and the divorce was inevitable. Contrary to popular belief, miracles do happen and they happen all the time. When did you observe your last miracle?

BE BRAVE

Did I forget to mention that you must also be brave? At the age of 12 I had my first introduction to bravery, emotional bravery. One afternoon coming home after helping my oldest brother deliver his daily newspapers, we approached the home I have lived in my entire life in total shock. All of our possessions were laid out on the curb in front of our house. We were homeless. I never looked at it as being homeless until I started thinking about how I would express my boldness here. I didn't think of us as being homeless because I was very busy trying to figure out how to deal with the embarrassment that was flooding my young mind. All I could think of was that our family was put out on the street, and I had to face my friends and schoolmates. It was as though the bed covers had been snatched off, and I was cold and the covers were nowhere to be found. This happening in the late 1950s was not nearly as prevalent as it is today. So, yes you must also be brave. Being brave for me meant just letting go, because there wasn't anything to hold on to. All we could do was move on.

Be Bold, Be Beautiful, Be Authentic is, on the surface, asking quite a lot of ourselves. In fact, it is pretty much asking for the impossible in the fast paced world we live in today. Really, who can find the time to address their boldness, beauty (inside and out) and be authentic? And let's not forget to be brave. You can!

One small bold step at a time and you're moving yourself closer to how you imagine your life to look and feel. You are unique and the first to recognize how beautiful you are from the inside out. You are the real deal and you know it. You are a work in progress, so there's no rush. You're authentic. You're learning to live life without conflict. You're brave enough to let go of what no longer serves you. Let's face it: You're Bold, You're Beautiful, You're Authentically You!

$\mathcal{C}$ONCLUSION

Well I told you, Bold is Beautiful. Did you gasp for air, laugh or cry? This is what it takes to show up, be strong and move forward to change your life.

I hope you take away at least one golden nugget, if not multiple golden nuggets, for your to strengthen your steps toward boldness. The world is waiting for you, trust me, I know!

I pondered on how to write this conclusion for quite some time, months in fact, and I asked myself over and over again, what do I want the readers to take away from *Bold is Beautiful*? And it comes back to me again and again: **anything is possible**. When you believe in yourself, you will thrive.

Women have voices, and these voices have been silenced over centuries in so many ways. I don't just mean your actual voice; I mean the voice in your heart, the voice in your gut and the voice that communicates with you from the universe. This has been shut down, turned off and completely ignored; it is now time to talk your heart's desires.

Walk, be bold and definitely beautiful! When you look deep into the mirror you will see YOU! The bold you waiting who's not afraid to step up, with no worries about what others think about you. Keep looking because there you will find courage, resilience, beauty, hope and dreams! A beautiful, confident and miraculous woman, standing right there. Reconnect with her, she is waiting!

In conclusion, I request – no, I demand you to go after those dreams and don't let YOU or anyone else take them away. The world is waiting!

Bold is Beautiful!

DO YOU DREAM OF HOSTING YOUR OWN RADIO SHOW?

I really love supporting women from around the world. This is what I do in my business: I collaborate with other women and support them in organizing their very own radio show! I help them get their voice out to the world, strengthen their expertise and market their business – all through radio.

Without a doubt, as business owners we need to increase our visibility, market and sell our businesses. A quick way to do this is through radio with your own show.

Do you want to turn your dream into a reality? Get in touch with me and I will show how to have a stress and worry-free, no technology expertise involved show; just get a phone and dial in. I handle everything from A to Z for you and your radio show.

Sounds exciting? Then email me at:

kim@kimboudreausmith.com

Here is to your Bold & Beautiful Self!

– Kim Boudreau Smith